The
Shih Tzu
Handbook

Sharon L. Vanderlip, D.V.M.

Filled with Full-color Photographs
Illustrations by Michele Earle-Bridges

BARRON'S

Acknowledgments

I would like to thank my husband, Jack Vanderlip, D.V.M., for his invaluable help as an expert consultant, his thoughts and ideas, and for reviewing the manuscript. Thanks to our daughter, Jacquelynn, for taking care of "the animals at home," so I would have more time to write. Thank you to Dr. Dan Rice for his excellent evaluation and helpful suggestions. And finally, a big thank you to my editor, Mark Miele, for his suggestions, guidance, and professionalism.

Photo Credits

Kent and Donna Dannen: pages vi, 4, 11, 16, 32, 35, 40, 45 bottom, 46, 55, 56, 57, 58, 65, 66, 129, 131, 136 top, 149, 153; Norvia Behling: pages 2, 3, 5, 7, 10, 13, 18, 19, 21, 23, 25, 26, 34, 37, 38, 39, 43, 45 top, 47, 48, 51, 53, 59, 60, 64, 68, 70, 79, 80, 81, 94, 96, 98, 99, 100, 102, 104, 106, 109, 110, 117, 127, 133, 150 top, 150 bottom; Sharon L. Vanderlip: page 6; Isabelle Francais: pages 27, 31, 61, 78, 119, 145; Pets by Paulette: pages 71, 72, 73, 74, 75, 76, 87, 91, 124, 136 bottom, 140; Tara Darling: pages 132, 142, 143.

About the the Author

Sharon Vanderlip, D.V.M., has provided veterinary care to domestic and exotic animal species for more than 25 years. She has authored several books on dog breeds and animal care and published numerous articles for scientific, veterinary, and general reading audiences.

Dr. Vanderlip served as the Associate Director of Veterinary Services for the University of California at San Diego School of Medicine and collaborated on reproductive research projects with the Zoological Society of San Diego. She is former Chief of Veterinary Services for the National Aeronautics and Space Administration (NASA), and is a consultant in reproductive medicine for various research and wildlife projects. Her practice focuses on canine reproductive medicine. She has lectured at kennel clubs and veterinary associations throughout the United States and Europe on topics in canine and exotic animal medicine and is the recipient of various awards for her writing and dedication to animal health.

Cover Photos

All photos by Isabelle Francais.

All inquiries should be addressed to:
Barron's Educational Series, Inc.
250 Wireless Boulevard
Hauppauge, New York 11788
http://www.barronseduc.com

ISBN-13: 978-0-7641-2632-1
ISBN-10: 0-7641-2632-6

Library of Congress Catalog Card No. 2003045129

Library of Congress Cataloging-in-Publication Data

Vanderlip, Sharon Lynn.
  The Shih tzu handbook / Sharon L. Vanderlip.
     p. cm.
  Includes bibliographical references (p.).
  ISBN 0-7641-2632-6 (alk. paper)
    1. Shih tzu. I. Title.

SF429.S64V36 2004
636.76—dc22   2003045129

Printed in China
9 8 7 6 5 4

Important Note

This book is concerned with selecting, keeping, and raising Shih Tzus. The publisher and the author think it is important to point out that the advice and information for Shih Tzu maintenance apply to healthy, normally developed animals with good dispositions obtained from a reputable source. Anyone who acquires an adult dog or one from an animal shelter must consider that the animal may have behavioral problems and may, for example, bite without any visible provocation. Such anxiety biters are dangerous for the owner as well as the general public.

Caution is further advised in the association of children with dogs, in meetings with other dogs, and in exercising the dog without a leash.

Extraordinary efforts have been made by the author and the publisher to ensure that treatment recommendations are precise and in agreement with standards accepted at the time of publication. If your dog exhibits any signs of illness you should consult a veterinarian immediately.

The author and publisher assume no responsibility for and make no warranty with respect to the results that may be obtained from procedures cited. Neither the author nor the publisher shall be liable for any damage resulting from reliance on any information contained herein, whether with respect to procedures, or by reason of any misstatement, error, or omission contained in this work.

Contents

Chapter One
Shih Tzu History

Your fortune cookie reads "There is a Shih Tzu in your life." Could it be true? Remember the first time you ever saw a Shih Tzu? You were captivated. And now you can't stop thinking about this remarkable little dog. You wonder, "Who is this charismatic canine with the beautiful flowing coat and an aura of magic? Even its name sounds exotic! The Shih Tzu—what does it mean? And where does it come from? Could this be the perfect dog for me?"

We are about to begin a fascinating journey that will answer those questions and many more. You will learn what you want to know about the Shih Tzu and discover the qualities and characteristics of this unique breed. So let your imagination run free as we step back in time to faraway places and ancient civilizations. Slip back into hidden valleys and remote, misty mountains to find the imperial palaces of China and the religious temples of Tibet. There, more than 3,000 years ago, at the foot of religious leaders, Buddhist monks, and powerful rulers, proudly sat the ancestors of today's Shih Tzu.

"Lion Dogs"

The Shih Tzu (pronounced *sheed zoo*) is a charming, intelligent, regal little dog. It may be small in stature, but it never fails to make a big impression on everyone it meets. With its winning personality, luxurious coat, and elegant demeanor, this attractive canine draws admirers wherever it goes. And Shih Tzus are just the right size, too. At only 9 to 10 inches (22.8 to 25.4 cm) high at the shoulder and weighing only 9 to 16 pounds (4 to 7.2 kg), Shih Tzus fit in every home and on every lap.

Shih Tzu means "lion" in Chinese. For several hundreds of years, many Asiatic dogs were bred to resemble small lions. "Lion dogs" were small and bearded, had round heads, flat faces, short noses, large round eyes, square bodies, and short legs. Lions held great significance in the Buddhist religion. They were considered the sacred beasts of Buddha and it was said that Buddha tamed a lion and rode it. Legend also said a lion followed Buddha everywhere. In the same manner, it was said that "lion dogs" followed in Buddha's foot-

For centuries the Shih Tzu was considered a rare and precious treasure of religious significance in China. Today this extraordinary canine has captured the hearts and imaginations of dog lovers worldwide.

steps and it was believed that "lion dogs" housed the spirits of Buddhist monks.

Today the white blaze on a Shih Tzu's forehead is called the "Star of Buddha" and the dark markings across the back are said to resemble the saddle Buddha used to ride a lion. Through the years, dedicated Shih Tzu breeders have done their best to follow the Shih Tzu ideal standard to keep the breed similar in size and appearance to the treasured "lion dogs" of ancient times.

Ancestral Shadows

There are hundreds of breeds of dogs and every one of them, including the Shih Tzu, traces back to the same prehistoric carnivorous (meat-eating) relative, a creature called Hesperocyonines. The fossil record tells us that Hesperocyonines evolved in North America about 40 million years ago and resembled a cross between a weasel and a fox. Before Hesperocyonines became extinct 15 million years ago, it gave rise to various canine species.

During the next several million years, many canine species became extinct, such as the dire wolves *(Canis dirus),* large wolves that lived in North America during the Pleistocene era and died out as recently as 10,000 years ago. However, there are 35 living species of canids that still exist today (including foxes, wolves, coyotes, jackals, and dogs). All of these species originated and evolved in

North America and all are distant descendants of Hesperocyonines.

Approximately 7 million years ago many canid species migrated from North America to Asia. One theory is that this migration was facilitated by a land bridge that may have existed during that era. This was a time before dogs, as we know them, existed. Of course, no human was there to document the migration or to record how the different species continued to evolve, but we do know that the Shih Tzu's remote ancestors were among them. We can only wonder at the fascinating changes that took place over the ages. Looking at today's gentle, yet elegant Shih Tzu, it's hard to imagine wild, savage, primitive canines far back in the trunk of the breed's family tree.

Origin of the Breed

The Shih Tzu's entire history will always remain a mystery, but we are fortunate to have the fossil record to help us glimpse across millions of years and fill in some gaps. For example, fossils tell us that although dog ancestors evolved in North America, the brachycephalic (short-skulled, short-nosed, flat-faced) dog *breeds*, such as the Shih Tzu, Pug, and Pekingese, originated in Central Asia.

In addition to the fossil record, we have written history and legends to help us roughly piece together the last 3,500 years of the Shih Tzu's history. We also have meticulously maintained breeding records and pedigrees for more than 50 years.

Few dog breeds have such a well-documented and exciting history as the Shih Tzu. This little dog has a big story to tell.

Asian Roots

Dogs have been an important part of Asian life for thousands of years. Skeletal remains of dogs have been found in Asia dating back more than 3,000 years, to the Shang Dynasty (1480 to 1050 B.C.). Many historians believe that the Asiatic dog breeds

Dogs with short skulls, flat faces, and short noses are called brachycephalic. Shih Tzus, Pugs, and Pekingese are closely related brachycephalic breeds that originated in Central Asia.

originated in Tibet and reached China as early as 1,400 years ago, probably by way of the Silk Trade Route, a route of more than 4,000 miles along the Great Wall of China from Sian, the capital of the Chinese Empire, over the Parmirs Mountains, and across Afghanistan. The Chinese traded silk in exchange for pet dogs. In addition, Dalai Lamas gave "holy dogs" and "lion dogs" to dignitaries of the Chinese imperial courts as diplomatic gifts and tributes during the Ch'ing dynasty, or Manchu dynasty (1644–1911).

Although lions are not native to China, the lion was considered Buddha's sacred and most important beast. The Chinese imperial courts began importing lions more than 2,000 years ago and "lion dogs" became especially popular in the Imperial Palace during the Manchu

From the Great Wall of China to your private garden wall, your Shih Tzu's history began thousands of miles away and spans thousands of years.

Dynasty. Because they were so low to the ground, "lion dogs" were often called "under the table dogs." Various "under the table dogs" were bred in China for 3,000 years. The Shih Tzu is not mentioned by name in the literature until the late fourteenth century.

There are several types of "lion dogs," including the Shih Tzu, Lhasa Apso, Pug, and Japanese Chin. The Shih Tzu was sometimes called the "chrysanthemum-faced dog" because of the way its hair grows out of its flat, round face in all directions, like a flower. "Lion dogs" were sometimes referred to as "sleeve dogs" because they fit, and could be carried about, in the large sleeves that were the fashion of the elite in China. They were also sometimes called "Fu dogs" (or "Foo dogs"), after a lionlike creature seen in art forms. The name was derived from a pair of dogs given to the Chinese court during the Tang dynasty in A.D. 624 that were believed to have come from Fu Lin, Turkey (Byzantine Empire).

In China, breeding and raising "lion dogs" was the responsibility of the eunuchs of the imperial courts. They competed to produce and raise the most attractive dogs. The best specimens were painted in the imperial dog books or on tapestries. Having one's animal painted was an honor and a great compliment. Eunuchs who produced the best dogs were rewarded with gifts from the emperor.

"Lion dogs" were considered to bring good luck. In addition to participating in regal processions and following at the heels of emperors and empresses, "lion dogs" reportedly guarded Buddhist temples, barking at would-be intruders. It was against the law to sell any of these royal dogs; to do so was punishable by death.

Holy Dogs

In Tibet, where the "cult of the lion" may have preceded that of China by several hundred years, Dalai Lamas kept "holy dogs" (the ancestors of Lhasa Apsos) in monasteries for centuries. The Dalai Lama was believed to be a reincarnation of Buddha and Tibetan monks were devoted to breeding "holy dogs" to resemble lions as much as possible.

It has been reported that around 1650 the Dalai Lama visited China and brought along three "holy dogs" from a temple in Tibet. Some researchers believe that these three "holy dogs" may have been interbred with Pekingese to create offspring with shorter muzzles, broader heads, and shorter legs and that these three animals are the foundation of today's Shih Tzu breed.

Predecessors

Some people think that the Shih Tzu was created by crossing Lhasa Apsos with Pekingese; others adamantly disagree. Another theory is that the Tibetan Spaniel may have been bred with the Pekingese to create the predecessor of the Shih Tzu and suggests that the Tibetan Spaniel is more similar to the Shih Tzu in conformation and temperament than is

Shih Tzus were also known as the "chrysanthemum-faced" dog because of the way hair grows out from the center of the flat, round face, like petals on a flower.

the Pekingese. Many believe that the Shih Tzu developed centuries ago in Tibet and reached China originally as a pure breed. Whatever the answer, it eludes us today. Perhaps in the future, with sophisticated scientific techniques such as polymerase chain

Shih Tzu Titles Through the Ages

Lion dog
Holy dog
Fu dog
Chrysanthemum-faced dog
Sleeve dog
Under the table dog
Shih Tzu Kou
Lhasa Lion Dog
Lhasa Terrier
Tibetan Poodle
Shock Dog

The "Foo dog" is a lion-like creature seen in ancient Chinese art forms.

reaction (PCR) and DNA analysis, the Shih Tzu's most contested secret may be revealed.

No matter what its exact beginnings are, there is no doubt that the Shih Tzu is the result of interbreeding original Tibetan "holy dogs" and various "lion dogs" in China. It is

Under that beautiful, flowing coat is a sturdy, compact body.

generally accepted that the oldest and smallest of the "holy dogs" are the ancestors of today's Shih Tzu.

Fight for Survival

As civil upheaval and war dominated the political picture in Asia, the Shih Tzu joined the list of tragic casualties. By 1750 "lion dogs" no longer existed in Tibet and were essentially limited to the imperial palace in Peking. By contrast, in Europe and the United States, almost 400 different dog breeds had already been established, dog shows had gained in popularity, and owning a purebred dog was considered a status symbol. By 1884 the American Kennel Club was founded and was soon registering thousands of dogs a year—yet there wasn't a Shih Tzu among them.

In 1908 the thirteenth Dalai Lama gave the Empress of China (Dowager Empress T'Zu His) some Shih Tzu-type dogs. She became enamored with the little canines and instructed the court eunuchs to maintain a breeding colony of them for many years. The Dowager Empress was the most powerful political figure in China in the late 1800s and early 1900s. She was a cruel dictator. Ironically, despite her tyrannical behavior, she had a soft spot in her heart for the Shih Tzu and was the person who most influenced the development of the breed. After her death in 1908, the imperial court dogs were sold to wealthy individu-

Meet a face sweet enough to soften the hardest of hearts. The Empress of China was a cruel dictator, but she loved the Shih Tzu-type dogs that she received as gifts from the thirteenth Dalai Lama. She is the person most responsible for the development of the Shih Tzu breed.

als or given away as gifts to foreign dignitaries and visitors. Some of these dogs were bred according to their appearance and type, but a formal registry or breed book was not maintained. Dogs that looked like Shih Tzus and Lhasa Apsos were grouped together and given several names: Shih Tzu, Shih Tzu Kou, Lion Dog, Lhasa Lion Dog, Apso, Holy Dog, and Lhasa Terrier.

The China Kennel Club was formed in 1923 but there was no breed standard, description, or registration. Without breed guidelines, it was difficult to judge Shih Tzu-type dogs. In 1934 the Peking Kennel Club was formed. The club hosted a dog show and held a class in which

Lhasa Lion Dogs could compete. Once again, the same judging difficulties were encountered. There was too much variation in size and appearance among the animals. Finally, a long-overdue standard was drawn up in 1938 describing the ideal "Shih Tzu Lion Dog."

Tragically, the following years were disastrous for the Shih Tzu breed. The Communists invaded Peking in 1949 and dog breeding in China came to an end. Fortunately, a British diplomat was able to import a few Shih Tzus into the United Kingdom in 1949. The last Shih Tzu recorded to leave China arrived in England in 1952, just before the remaining animals were destroyed by

Peking Kennel Club Official Shih Tzu Standard 1938–

List of Desired Shih Tzu Characteristics
- Lion head with long, heart-shaped ears and long hair on the ears
- Skull broad and flat
- Long hair on the hind legs
- Large eyes, covered completely by hair
- Paws broad and flat, covered with hair
- Tail carried over the back
- All colors allowed, but honey color is a favorite
- 13–15 inches (33–38 cm) tall at the shoulders
- 10–15 pounds (4.5–6.8 kg)

the Communist Revolution that led to the extinction of the Shih Tzu in Asia. The foundation of the Shih Tzu breed, as we know it today, comes primarily from the few Shih Tzus that were imported into the U.K. in the 1900s.

A Second Chance

During the 1930s a few Shih Tzu were exported to England, Ireland, and Scandinavia, primarily through the efforts of Mrs. Douglas Brownrigg (the wife of a general) of England and Miss Madelaine Hutchins of Ireland. These two women were enthusiastic pioneers in promoting the Shih Tzu and exhibited their dogs at as many shows as possible. In those days, Shih Tzus were called Tibetan Lion Dogs, or Apsos, and lumped together in the show ring with Lhasa Apsos (known at that time as Tibetan Apsos). Eventually, dog fanciers were able to convince the Kennel Club that the Shih Tzu and Lhasa Apso were two different breeds with very distinctive traits. In 1934 a Shih Tzu club was formed in the United Kingdom and even Queen Elizabeth took a special interest in the mysterious breed from across the globe.

The British Kennel Club had registered 183 Shih Tzus by 1939, but this brief resurgence would not last. Barely had the Shih Tzu returned from near extinction when it was once again set back by the fury of war. During World War II almost all breeding, exhibiting, competing, and importing of the Shih Tzu (and most other dogs in Europe, for that matter) came to an immediate halt. Even wealthy people did not have money, space, or time for the extravagance of a dog hobby during the war. Shih Tzus numbered 61 between 1940 and 1947 and only two new Shih Tzus were registered with the Kennel Club of England in 1945.

A Limited Gene Pool

After World War II, there were very few Shih Tzus in Europe. A few had reached the U.K. from China in 1948,

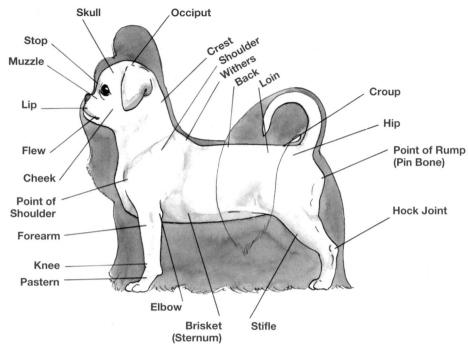

Skull Occiput

Stop

Muzzle

Crest Shoulder

Withers

Back Loin

Lip

Croup

Hip

Flew

Point of Rump
(Pin Bone)

Cheek

Point of
Shoulder

Hock Joint

Forearm

Knee

Pastern

Elbow

Brisket
(Sternum) Stifle

Parts of a Shih Tzu's body.

but by 1952 the Shih Tzu no longer existed in China. Of the few animals left in the U.K., many seemed to have medical problems or died at an early age. Perhaps the problems were caused by disease, or poor housing conditions, or insufficient food during wartime—but what if the problems were hereditary? What if the Shih Tzu breed was becoming weak because there was not enough genetic diversity and all the Shih Tzus were too closely related? How could the breed be saved? What could a breeder do?

Breeders decided that they would breed as many remaining Shih Tzus as possible. They would not remove an animal from the breeding program just because it wasn't a perfect specimen of the breed. Even dogs that didn't look like "ideal" Shih Tzus would be used for breeding because there just weren't enough animals in existence to allow a breeder to be too critical or too discriminating. As a result, the Shih Tzu increased in size and weight and became larger than the original Shih Tzu from China.

In 1952 Elfreda Evans, a dog fancier relatively new to the Shih Tzu community, did the unthinkable. She deliberately bred a Shih Tzu to a Pekingese. She believed her actions

Shih Tzus suffered the effects of World War II. Only two new Shih Tzus were registered in the United Kingdom in 1945.

were justified because there were too few Shih Tzus available to breed and they were too inbred. She also believed that because the dogs were so closely related they were developing too many faults. Mrs. Evans thought that by crossing a Shih Tzu with a Pekingese (a breed that some people thought may have previously been crossed with Shih Tzus by eunuchs in the imperial palaces of China), she could reduce the size of the Shih Tzu breed and also improve bone structure and the appearance of the muzzle. (It is true that size was becoming a concern. In 1962 the Manchu Shih Tzu Society began efforts to reduce the size of the Shih Tzu back to 10 pounds (4.5 kg), the original size of Shih Tzus housed in the imperial palaces.)

Pekingese Cross

What did Mrs. Evans do with the mongrel (mixed breed) offspring from the Shih Tzu/Pekingese cross? She bred them to purebred Shih Tzus. This second generation of puppies was now genetically three-quarters Shih Tzu and one-quarter Pekingese. She then mated these animals to purebred Shih Tzus, and so on. The Pekingese was no longer used for matings to Shih Tzus and was not introduced into any subsequent generations.

Understandably, Mrs. Evans' actions sparked controversy, met with disagreement, and were severely criticized by many. Outcrossing the Shih Tzu to a different breed caused a setback, making it more difficult for the Shih Tzu to gain acceptance as a breed in its own right. Shih Tzus that were descendants of the Shih Tzu/Pekingese cross were recorded as such in the Kennel Club records. The Kennel Club would not recognize any of the descendants of the Shih Tzu/Pekingese outcross as purebred Shih Tzu until they were at least four generations removed from the original Shih Tzu/Pekingese mating.

Not all of today's Shih Tzu's are descendants of Mrs. Evans' breeding endeavors. Other breeders chose to limit their breeding to Shih Tzus only, no matter how limited the gene pool. Unfortunately, descendants from pure Shih Tzu only lines are rare today.

Did Mrs. Evans have a good idea? Were her efforts successful? Did she contribute to the improvement of the breed? Even today, not all Shih Tzu experts agree. As a Shih Tzu enthusiast, you are invited to review the many pedigrees and photographs of the era and judge for yourself. (Books that discuss the history of the Shih Tzu in greater detail are listed under Useful Addresses and Literature at the back of this book.) We do know, however, that by 1966 there were 15 registered Shih Tzu champions in the United Kingdom that were descendants of Mrs. Evans' Shih Tzu/Pekingese cross.

One of the greatest moments in Shih Tzu history was in 1963, when a Shih Tzu named Champion Elling-ham Kala Nag won Best of Breed at Crufts, the most renowned and respected dog show in the United Kingdom. The exotic breed with the long and turbulent history had survived all odds. The Shih Tzu was well on its way to winning hearts around the world.

Full Circle

In the truest of senses, the Shih Tzu had come full circle when it reached the United States in 1938. It had returned to the continent of its most ancient and primitive ancestors—the continent they had abandoned for Asia, seven million years ago.

In the beginning, a few Shih Tzus were imported from China, but these

A welcome flower in any garden, the chrysanthemum-faced dog has returned from the brink of extinction several times.

animals usually had no known pedigree, other than perhaps one generation (the parents). Most of the first Shih Tzu imports were brought to the United States by military personnel who had been stationed in the U.K. during World War II. Throughout the 1950s Americans continued to purchase and import their Shih Tzus from breeders in the U.K.

In spite of its appeal and distinctive appearance, and the formation of a Shih Tzu breed club in 1938, it was a long time before the Shih Tzu received breed recognition from the American Kennel Club (AKC). In the beginning, Shih Tzus could be listed only as and exhibited with Lhasa Apsos. When the AKC finally accepted the Shih Tzu as a distinct breed in 1955, it was listed as a member of the Miscellaneous Class. This change in status allowed the Shih Tzu to compete for awards in obedience trials but still did not allow Shih Tzus to compete in conformation (beauty according to a set standard) classes. In 1957 the Shih Tzu made its debut at a dog show in Philadelphia. It was a small step, but a significant moment in Shih Tzu history. No one would ever forget the charismatic little "lion dog" that represented its ancient breed that day.

Spurred on by their successes, Shih Tzu breeders worked hard to achieve AKC recognition. By 1960 there were three Shih Tzu clubs: the Texas Shih Tzu Society, the Shih Tzu Club of America, and the American Shih Tzu Association. In 1963, the Texas Shih Tzu Society and the Shih

Tzu Club of America united to form the American Shih Tzu Club and by 1964 there were approximately 400 Shih Tzus registered in the United States.

Although much progress had been made, Shih Tzu fanciers in the United States continued to face a difficult dilemma. There were no animals available to import from China, and the AKC would not recognize or register any Shih Tzu that was not at least six generations removed from Mrs. Evans' 1952 Shih Tzu/Pekingese cross (more than the four generations the Kennel Club of England required). There were very few Shih Tzus in the country, although interest in the breed had grown considerably. For a while, it seemed that the Shih Tzu would never gain a solid foothold in America.

A Success Story

Shih Tzu enthusiasts were thrilled when at long last the breed received AKC recognition. It was the goal everyone had worked toward and it was the boost the breed needed to succeed. The AKC admitted the Shih Tzu for registration in the AKC Stud Book in March 1969, and to regular show classification in the Toy Group at AKC shows on September 1, 1969. On that same day in September, Shih Tzu Champion Chumulari Ying-Ying won Best in Show in New Jersey against keen competition and 970 other dogs, while his father, Champion Bjorneholms Pif, won the

Toy Group in Illinois. At the same time, across the continent, a female Shih Tzu named Lakoya Princess Tanya Shu won the Toy Group in Oregon. Thirty-eight years had passed from the time the first Shih Tzu club formed to the time the breed was admitted for registration in the AKC Stud Book. After so many years and so much hard work, suddenly the Shih Tzu became a sensation overnight. The victories mounted as the first Shih Tzus exhibited in conformation classes in 1969 won their championship titles in less than a month and the breed's popularity soared. In that same year the AKC officially registered approximately 3,000 Shih Tzus. Clearly the Shih Tzu had won more than trophies and ribbons—it had won a permanent place in America's heart!

By 1980 the Shih Tzu population had skyrocketed into the thousands and Shih Tzus were being exported to many countries around the world and in 1989 the American Shih Tzu Club (ASTC) developed a more descriptive standard to guide Shih Tzu breeders (see page 14).

Today, in the United States, the Shih Tzu ranks among the ten most popular breeds (out of 150 breeds recognized by the AKC) and Shih Tzu puppy registrations range between

Your Shih Tzu's exotic appearance is the result of hundreds of generations of selective breeding.

an astounding 30,000 and 40,000 every year.

Seven dogs (males) and seven bitches (females) are reportedly behind the entire gene pool of all Shih Tzus in existence today. Surprisingly, most Shih Tzus today are distant descendants of the Pekingese dog used in the controversial Shih Tzu/Pekingese cross in 1952. There is a very limited number of Shih Tzus in existence that are distinct, or free, of the Shih Tzu/Pekingese cross. Without a dedicated effort to preserve and maintain the Peke-free lineage, it could be permanently lost.

Chapter Two

Today's Shih Tzu

The Shih Tzu Standard

A Shih Tzu's personality is as important as its endearing appearance. That is why Shih Tzu temperament is included and described in the official AKC standard. A Shih Tzu is first and foremost a housepet and a companion. It should always be outgoing, happy, friendly, affectionate, and trusting toward everyone. Serious faults in personality include aggression, nervousness, or shyness. A Shih Tzu should be alert and lively and carry itself in a proud, arrogant, aristocratic manner with its head held high and its tail curved over its back.

Color: Shih Tzus come in a variety of colors and markings, ranging from golden to black. All colors are permissible and no color is considered more desirable than another. Color is simply a matter of personal preference. (Some coat colors may change as the animal ages.) The animal's overall quality is much more important than its color.

Coat: The coat should be luxurious, dense, double-coated, long, and flowing. Hair should not be curly, but a slight wave to the coat is all right.

Size: Size ranges from 9 to 10½ inches (22.6–26.6 cm) at the shoulders, females usually being smaller than males. A Shih Tzu should not be taller than 11 inches (28 cm) or shorter than 8 inches (20.3 cm). Ideal weight is from 9 to 16 pounds (4–7.2 kg) and should be in proportion to the animal. The Shih Tzu is a compact, solid, sturdy dog. It should never appear squatty or leggy, but it should be low to the ground. A nicely balanced Shih Tzu is slightly longer than it is tall.

Head: One of the most distinguishing features of the Shih Tzu is its round, broad, domed head. There should be a lot of space between the eyes. A narrow head or close-set eye placement is considered a fault in the breed. They detract from the warmth and sweetness of expression for which the Shih Tzu is recognized. A beautiful Shih Tzu always has a wide-eyed, friendly, and trusting appearance. Large, expressive, round, dark eyes are preferred. It's important to look under the hair to see the eyes, face, and true expression of the animal.

There is a definite stop to the muzzle. The muzzle is set no lower than the bottom eyelids and is square and unwrinkled. The muzzle is short and ideally no longer than 1 inch (2.54 cm) from the tip of the nose to the stop (although larger dogs may have slightly longer muzzles). The broad nostrils are wide and open and not pinched shut. Large, heavily coated ears are set slightly below the crown of the skull. The Shih Tzu's jaw is broad and wide and the lips should meet evenly. The teeth and tongue should not be visible when the mouth is closed. A missing tooth or slightly misaligned teeth are not uncommon.

General appearance: The Shih Tzu is an aristocratic, noble dog. Its well-balanced appearance is characteristic of the breed. The neck should be long enough to allow the animal to carry its head high and be in balance with its height and body length. The back, or topline, should be level and the body should be sturdy. The chest is deep with ribs well sprung. The tail is set high, carried over the back, like a "teapot handle," and heavily plumed (covered with lots of long, thick hair). Legs are straight, strong, and well muscled. Short hocks provide greater drive in the hindquarters. Feet should point straight ahead. Dewclaw removal is optional.

Movement: Movement, or gait, is extremely important in the Shih Tzu. Movement should appear smooth and effortless, as though the animal were flowing. The graceful, fluid gait of the

A Kaleidoscope of Colors

Shih Tzus come in a wide variety of colors and all colors are acceptable! The only rule is that noses, lips, and eyelid margins must be black and eyes should be dark. Of course, there are exceptions to most rules. If your Shih Tzu is liver- or blue-colored, then the pigmentation must compliment the color. Very fashionable!

So, are you ready to add a little color to your life? Here's a partial list of some Shih Tzu colors.
• Gold
• Gold and white
• Cream
• Deep red
• Red and white
• Grizzle gray
• Silver and white
• Brindle
• Liver (with light eyes and brown nose)
• Blue (with blue eyes and slate blue nose)
• Black-masked
• Black tips
• Solid black
• Black and white
• Saddle markings
• White blaze

No matter what color you prefer, remember that health and personality are much more important than color. Never buy a puppy based on color alone or as first consideration.

American Kennel Club Group Classifications

Group I	Sporting Dogs
Group II	Hounds
Group III	Working Dogs
Group IV	Terriers
Group V	Toys
Group VI	Non-Sporting Dogs
Group VII	Herding Dogs
Miscellaneous Class	

Group V: Toys

Affenpinscher	Miniature Pinscher
Brussels Griffon	Papillon
Chihuahua	Pekingese
Chinese Crested	Pomeranian
English Toy Spaniel	Poodle (Toy)
Italian Greyhound	Pug
Japanese Chin	Shih Tzu
Maltese	Silky Terrier
Manchester Terrier (Toy)	Yorkshire Terrier

Shih Tzus are known for their endearing appearance and trusting nature.

Shih Tzu is emphasized by a beautiful, properly groomed, flowing coat.

The Shih Tzu's Place in the Dog World

The Shih Tzu is a member of the Toy Group (AKC classification Group V) that includes several unusual dog breeds, including three other breeds from Asia: the Japanese Chin, the Pekingese, and the Pug. (Interestingly, the Lhasa Apso, with which the Shih Tzu was originally exhibited, belongs to the Non-Sporting group that includes the Tibetan Terrier and the Tibetan Spaniel.)

Chapter Three

Considerations Before You Buy

Is a Shih Tzu the Right Dog for You?

You meet a Shih Tzu for the first time and suddenly find yourself enchanted by this magical, mysterious, charismatic character. Its charm and confidence, endearing appearance, portable size, and alert countenance have an alluring appeal that sets it apart from all other canine breeds. You admire the attractive little dog's intelligence and are taken with its friendly, outgoing personality. What could be sweeter than a Shih Tzu's big eyes and warm, trusting expression? What could be more loving and affectionate than a Shih Tzu? You feel like your heart is melting. You want to take this cute, cuddly, wonderful creature home *right now*. But of course, common sense calls out to you: Don't buy on an impulse. There's responsibility to pet ownership. You know you must first do your homework to help you decide if a Shih Tzu would be a compatible companion. So let's get started.

A Constant Companion

There is a lot to learn about Shih Tzus and their care. First and foremost, Shih Tzus want to be with people as much as possible and do not like to be left alone. They have been bred throughout the centuries to be the quintessential companion, always at your side, always in your presence, craving love and attention nonstop. Do you have time for such a demanding personality? If you are walking, your Shih Tzu will follow or ask to be carried. If you sit down, your Shih Tzu will demand to be petted, coddled, snuggled, or held on your lap. If you are eating, your Shih Tzu will beg for a treat—don't give in (see more about treats and begging in the chapter on nutrition, Chapter Seven).

If you want a dog that is a constant shadow and if you have lots of time to stay home and play with your dog, then a Shih Tzu is a good candidate. By lots of time, we mean enough time every day to socialize, groom, and exercise your pet on a regular basis for several years, because Shih Tzus have long life spans. They can live 11 to 15 years or more, so the first thing you must decide is whether your lifestyles and personalities are compatible. Shih Tzus are wonderful dogs, but they are not for everyone.

Shih Tzu Shenanigans

Don't let the small size fool you. In the case of the Shih Tzu, small is synonymous with active, busy, curious, and creative. If you don't find toys and activities to entertain your little dog, it will find its own form of entertainment, including digging, chewing, barking, and exploring. If you plan on owning a Shih Tzu, you must also plan on having a well-fenced yard (for supervised exercise), doors that close securely, lots of toys and activities, and lots of time to exercise, socialize, train, and groom this dynamo of energy. And plan on sudden bursts of energy. The Shih Tzu may look like a decorative dog, and indeed it will embellish your life, but it is a mobile vortex much of the time. Be forewarned and be prepared!

Shih Tzus are good-natured, but vivacious. They may be intelligent, but they are not always easy to train. Shih Tzus thrive on human companionship and attention and this makes them easy to spoil. They sometimes show a stubborn streak, with just a touch of pride and arrogance. Add to this the fact that they have short attention spans, selective memories, and are easily distracted. They have a good sense of humor and would rather clown around than get serious and concentrate on a training session. The only way you can train your Shih Tzu to do what you want her to do, or to behave appropriately, is by making her *want* to cooperate. Plan on spending the time required to teach your little "lion dog" the basics (see page 135). Keep in mind that some lessons, such as house-training, may require several refresher courses.

Be realistic in your expectations. Although some Shih Tzus have won various high level obedience titles, yours may never join their ranks. That is not to say your canine can't go far beyond the basics; after all, she's definitely smart enough. But keep in mind that Shih Tzus were bred to be

It's easy to fall in love with a Shih Tzu puppy, but make sure a Shih Tzu is right for you before you bring one home!

ornamental companions, not working dogs. Some Shih Tzus excel at obedience work, but that's not without the patience, skills, and talent of their dedicated, experienced owners. It's not easy to keep a Shih Tzu focused, and although a Shih Tzu can easily learn house manners, perfecting obedience work is definitely a challenge.

Your Shih Tzu may enjoy entertaining you by obeying a few commands, but when the novelty wears off and she tires of the activity, she wants to be catered to and coddled. If you ask for a repeat performance, she may stubbornly refuse and all the cajoling in the world won't work. A Shih Tzu has a mind of its own so don't set your bar of expectations too high. Then, if you are a successful trainer and your dog has a love for obedience work, you'll both be pleasantly surprised!

Your Home Is a Palace

The Shih Tzu is a palace-dweller. For thousands of years its residences included such haughty addresses as imperial palaces, chez Dalai Lama, and top political figures' and dignitaries' homes. To your small companion, your safe and cozy home is also a palace. With a comfortable place to sleep, excellent care, good food, and a loving family, your dog could not be happier.

Today, the Shih Tzu remains strictly a housepet, just as it was

Shih Tzus are active and curious. Be sure your pet has activities and toys to keep it busy when you are not home.

centuries ago. Shih Tzus cannot tolerate harsh weather, especially the heat. The brachycephalic (pushed-in and flattened) face and the long, flowing coat make it somewhat difficult to breathe and to tolerate temperature extremes. Shih Tzus need good ventilation, fresh air, and a cool, protected area.

Exercise: All dogs require daily exercise, and the Shih Tzu is no exception. Although the Shih Tzu should always be a housepet, it requires exercise just like any other dog. A daily walk on a leash, or a romp in the yard, will help keep your companion physically fit and in good health, but you must be there to supervise and coordinate activities. Your pet won't work out on her own, but she will miss you and possibly try to escape from the yard if you're not there. Never leave your Shih Tzu unsupervised in the backyard and, whatever you do, *never leave your pet alone outside or tied to a tree or a post in the backyard.*

Outdoors: Life outdoors is also incompatible with your pet's coat type. It would be almost impossible to groom and keep the coat in top condition. You would spend hours every week just trying to maintain some sense of order among the tangles, burrs, grass awns, dirt, parasites, and mats. So, if you are unable to house your dog indoors, do not even think of owning a Shih Tzu—an outdoor lifestyle is out of the question! Whether you live in a palace or an apartment, your Shih Tzu should live there (*indoors*), too!

Never leave your Shih Tzu in the yard unattended. Check for holes in and under the fence and areas where your pet can escape.

Hair Everywhere

Shih Tzus may be small, but they have a lot of hair! You will have to set aside lots of time for regular grooming sessions (see Grooming Your Shih Tzu, Chapter Six), to keep your Shih Tzu's skin and coat healthy.

All dogs shed sometime during the year. Although Shih Tzus are considered by some to shed less and to be less allergenic (allergenic means likely to cause allergies) than many other breeds, they *do* shed. If you groom your companion daily, shedding should not be significant. Most of the shed and broken hairs will end up in the hairbrush and not on your clothing or the furniture.

A well-groomed Shih Tzu is nothing less than stunning and attracts admirers like a magnet. Just wait until you go for a walk with your pet. You'll see!

The Commitment

Whether to bring a new dog into your life, and when to do it, are major decisions that require serious consideration before you take action. Dog ownership is both a joy and a serious responsibility. During the years, your companion will rely on you for love, attention, proper nutrition, grooming, exercise, training, and good health care. To satisfy these requirements, you must be prepared for the financial aspects of responsible pet ownership, as well as for the investments you cannot really measure: time and emotion.

Your Shih Tzu's ancestors lived in palaces. No wonder your pet enjoys living indoors and resting on comfortable furniture.

The Best Time to Acquire a Shih Tzu

You have made your decision and your heart is set on a Shih Tzu. Now you need to think about the best time to introduce one into your life and your home. You may want a Shih Tzu right now, but there may be circumstances that prevent you from fulfilling this dream immediately. It is not always easy to find the perfect dog right away. Start contacting breeders now so you can be placed on their waiting list. Sometimes it's hard to be patient, but in the end you will find a Shih Tzu that is ideal for you and you won't be disappointed.

If you have too many obligations right now, postpone your purchase until you have the time to give your Shih Tzu the care and attention it deserves. Shih Tzus are bright, active, and loving. They thrive on your company and affection, and will become bored and depressed when left all alone, especially for long periods of time. Lonely dogs and puppies often get into mischief and that's when good dogs turn bad. If your Shih Tzu has nothing to do and you aren't there to keep it company, it can develop unwanted behaviors, including barking, chewing, digging, destroying objects, and trying to escape. If it becomes very sad it may lose interest in its surroundings and stop eating.

A Quick Quiz

Every Shih Tzu has its own unique personality, but there are distinct behavioral and inherited (genetic) traits distinctive of the breed—traits that are deeply engrained in these gentle-natured little dogs. The characteristics that have made the Shih Tzu a treasured pet for religious leaders and imperial families of Tibet and China for centuries are the same ones that make the Shih Tzu a precious companion today. They include an alert and outgoing personality, a beautiful coat, and an extremely affectionate nature. Shih Tzus love everyone. Your Shih Tzu will want to be with you every chance it can, so if you are planning on bringing a Shih Tzu into your life, be sure you will have a lot of time to spend with it!

Here's a little quiz to help you determine if a Shih Tzu is the right dog for you.

1. Do you enjoy the company of a dog that is beautiful, elegant, and portable?

2. Are you looking for a dog that is gentle and affectionate?

3. Do you have a lot of time and love to give to a little dog that craves attention, loves pampering, and wants to be part of every family activity?

4. Can you afford to feed your dog quality food and provide it with veterinary care?

5. Will you be able to adjust your schedule so you can exercise your dog every day?

6. Do you have the desire and time to groom your dog, or can you afford to pay a professional groomer to do the job on a regular basis?

7. Do you have the patience and understanding to train your companion?

If you have answered "yes" to these questions, then you just might be ready to join the ranks of thousands of people who have owned and loved Shih Tzus!

If you are moving or changing jobs, a new pet will probably be added stress rather than enjoyment. If you are planning a vacation soon, you will have to make arrangements for animal care in your absence. Rather than stress your new companion by a change in environment and caregivers, it is best to wait until you return from vacation before you introduce a new dog into your home.

We all have seen the movies, animations, and advertisements in which a young puppy is wrapped up in bows sitting by the fireplace as a surprise holiday gift. There are two things wrong with this concept: First, it is unwise to buy a pet for someone else. Pet ownership is a responsibility not everyone wants to assume. If a person wants a new dog, you can bet that person would prefer to

choose the animal, rather than have someone else make that decision. Second, adding a new pet to the family during the holiday season should be discouraged. This is a time when most people already have more than enough to do with visitors and commitments. New pets often are overlooked in the busy holiday shuffle with all the distractions and excitement. Families cannot take the time out during the holidays to learn about, supervise, socialize, and care for a new animal. Visitors and guests may stress, frighten, or mishandle the new dog. They may even be bitten. Someone may forget to close the kennel, a door, or a fence gate and your new friend may escape, be lost or injured, or even killed by a moving vehicle. In the holiday confusion, your Shih Tzu could miss a meal, or be overfed, unless someone is specifically assigned the responsibility of feeding. Finally, dogs purchased and transported (especially in cold weather) during the holidays may be more stressed or prone to illness than usual. Shih Tzus do not tolerate harsh weather conditions or temperature extremes. They are strictly housedogs and should never be left outdoors in bad weather. To prevent stress to yourself and to your new canine companion, wait until the holidays are over before you buy a new dog and bring it home.

Household Pets

Your Shih Tzu (let's call her "Cookie") is full of energy and curiosity. She has a keen sense of smell and is interested in meeting all the new members of your family, including other household pets. Make sure the introductions are done slowly and safely. For example, if you own another dog or a cat, don't expect them to be friends right from the beginning. Your other pets will be cautious and possibly jealous of the newcomer. A resentful cat can inflict serious injury on an unsuspecting dog, especially a tiny puppy. Eye injuries from cat scratches are common accidents experienced by dogs. And if you have another dog in the

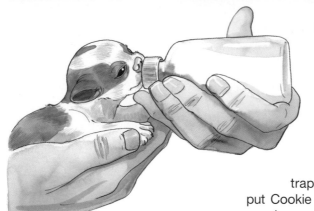

Your new puppy should be completely weaned and able to eat on its own before it leaves its mother. Bottle-feeding is necessary for orphans, or puppies whose mother is unable to produce enough milk. A special formula can be purchased from pet stores and veterinarians.

home, remember that it may be jealous of the attention you are giving Cookie, particularly if your dog is an adult or aged animal. Even if your pets are happy to have Cookie join the family, be sure that they do not play too roughly and accidentally injure her. Adult Shih Tzus may be sturdy little dogs, but a little puppy can be very fragile.

Introducing the New Puppy

A good way to start introductions in the family is to place Cookie in an area of the home where she is safe from other animals, but where they can observe and smell each other. For example, if you have a laundry area, or space next to the kitchen, you can place a baby barrier gate there to prevent the new arrival from running loose in the house without your permission until she adapts to her new environment and your other pets are used to her. Make sure the barrier has a mesh small enough to prevent escape or accidental injury and that Cookie cannot become

trapped in it. You may also put Cookie in her crate the first few evenings so that your other household animals can approach and investigate, but cannot harm her. Remember to pay extra attention to your established pets so they are not jealous. It will be a real challenge juggling your attention among your pets and spreading your affection so that they all feel they have received their fair share, especially if your other pets are also Shih Tzus!

Aggression

In most cases, animals learn to live peacefully together in a household. In the very unlikely situation Cookie is aggressive toward other dogs, neutering (spaying or castrating) your dogs may help the problem. The results are best if your pets are neutered at a young age (see page 25). (Note: Signs of aggression are considered a serious fault in Shih Tzu character.)

Pets to Avoid

There are some household pets Cookie should never meet. These include any small mammals (such as mice, rats, hamsters, guinea pigs, rabbits, or ferrets), birds, or reptiles.

Although Shih Tzus were never bred for hunting, back in the recesses of their mind lie the instincts of primitive ancestors. Even if Cookie doesn't have the notion that these small animals are fair game, she may consider them fabulous toys and Shih Tzus can play rough. Small pets and birds sense when there is a dog in the area and will be frightened and stressed if their cage is approached. Shih Tzus are very clever and very quick! Make sure the lid or door to your small pet's cage is securely fastened. Then place the cage where Cookie cannot find it. Remember, she has a good sense of smell and will easily find these animals, so don't just place them out of sight—make sure they are out of reach until you are absolutely certain they will all get along well together!

Shih Tzus are friendly and trusting, but sometimes friendships take time. To avoid injuries, never leave pets alone together until you know they are compatible.

Should Your Shih Tzu Be Neutered?

Preventive veterinary care is just as important as tender loving care. One of the most important health decisions you will make is whether to have Cookie spayed, or, if you have a male Shih Tzu (let's call him "Lotus"), to have him castrated. These procedures (called "gonadectomy" or "neutering") refer to the inactivation or removal of some, or all, of the tissues in the body associated with reproduction (testicles in the male, ovaries and uterus in the female).

Female Shih Tzus usually come into estrus (also called "in heat" or "in season") around the age of six months and cycle approximately every six months thereafter, depending on their family genetics. Ideally, your female should be spayed before her first estrous cycle, and certainly before her second estrous cycle, so that she will have a significantly reduced chance of developing mammary (breast) cancer later in life. If you wait until after the second estrous cycle, your pet will have almost as much chance of developing breast cancer than if she had not been spayed. Mammary cancer is common in older dogs, and 50 percent of mammary cancer in dogs is life-threatening. So, it makes good medical sense to neuter your pet at a very early age.

Puppies are cute, but raising Shih Tzus is difficult, time-consuming, and very expensive. It's also hard on the mother. To reduce medical risks, have your pet neutered.

Early surgical neutering can be performed safely on pups between six and sixteen weeks of age. Studies have shown that prepubertal gonadectomy (neutering before an animal is sexually mature) does not affect growth rate, food intake, or weight gain of growing dogs. In 1993 the American Veterinary Medical Association formally approved early neutering of dogs (and cats), a procedure many veterinarians and humane organizations had been promoting for many years.

There are distinct health advantages for dogs that are surgically neutered early in life. Early neutering:

1. greatly reduces the chance of developing mammary (breast) cancer if the ovaries are removed before the female's second, and preferably first, estrous cycle.

2. prevents ovarian, uterine, testicular, prostate, or epididymal diseases, such as cancer and infection.

3. prevents unwanted pregnancies.

4. leads to less surgical procedure time.

5. has a rapid recovery period (young, healthy animals heal quickly).

6. leads to fewer behavior problems.

7. eliminates the inconveniences associated with a female dog in estrus

Either a male or a female makes a wonderful companion. You may decide to have one of each! Be sure to have them neutered to prevent unwanted pregnancies.

(vaginal bleeding and discharge that can stain furniture and carpets and attract neighborhood dogs).

In addition to surgical neutering, pet owners now have the option of chemical neutering for male puppies. The world's first drug to neuter puppies was approved by the Food and Drug Administration in March 2003 and is now available. The drug (amino acid 1 arginine and a zinc salt) is injected directly into the testicles and causes atrophy (shrinkage) of the testicles and prostate gland. There are four disadvantages of this form of castration:

1. The injection must be administered in the correct place to avoid complications.

2. The animal requires follow-up care and observation to make sure there are no medical complications after treatment.

3. Testosterone (a sex hormone that can cause aggression in some males) secretion is not completely shut off, so the procedure does not help improve behavioral problems associated with aggression.

4. The price of the injection may be similar to the cost of a surgical castration for some animals.

No procedure is completely without risk or side effects. Your veterinarian will advise you about the benefits and possible risks of neutering your pet and the best technique to use.

Wrong Reasons to Breed Your Dog

- So that the children can experience "the wonder of life" and the birth process. Children are not always filled with as much "wonder" as parents think. Children can observe birth by watching any of the countless nature and science animal documentaries. The only "wonder" will be how a litter of puppies can eat and defecate so much, be so much hard work, and cost so much to raise—and you can bet the children won't be around to share that wonderment with you.
- So that your dog can experience the "joy of parenthood." Raising a litter is not a joyful experience for a dog. It's hard work and can affect the mother's health. She may need surgery or may develop a uterine or mammary infection or experience other health problems.
- So that you can make money from the sale of the puppies. When raised properly, the expenses of raising a litter of pups far exceeds the endless list of costs, including food, grooming products, housing, and veterinary care. Don't forget to add in your working hours as well. You won't even come close to earning your usual salary.
- So that your aging family dog "will have a friend." A new litter of pups can be very stressful for an aging animal. The older dog may be depressed about the extra attention the pups are receiving.
- So that you will have a dog just like the one you own now. Every puppy is a unique individual; a puppy is not a clone of either of its parents. If you are trying to duplicate a dog you already own, don't do it—you can never replace a dog with one exactly like it. You will be disappointed if the puppy doesn't meet your expectations.
- So that "its family line can be continued." Sixty years ago there were very few Shih Tzus in existence; today there are several thousands. Be honest. Do you really know all the genetics behind your dog? Does it have problems that could be hereditary? Is your dog really outstanding, or can the breed survive without its genetic contribution?

No matter what method you use, you can be assured that you are doing the right thing. You are giving your little friend the best chance for a long, healthy life and you are doing a community service by not contributing to the pet overpopulation problem. Statistics show that for every female dog that produces one litter of puppies, there is the potential to give rise to 67,000 descendents in a six-year time period. Does this sound incredible? Consider the fact that there are 30,000 to 40,000 Shih Tzus registered by the American Kennel Club every year in the United States and that these are planned matings from animals that were deliberately selected for breeding purposes. Add to that all the other Shih Tzus that are not registered and all the unintended breedings that happened "by accident."

After all the work you have done to find just the right Shih Tzu companion and give it the care it deserves, it may be hard to imagine that any Shih Tzu—a regal animal bred to live a pampered life of luxury in palatial estates—would end up in animal shelters, rejected, neglected, sick, and unwanted. Sadly, it's true. A Shih Tzu is not an easy dog to maintain. It requires a lot of personal attention and its coat requires frequent grooming. Some dogs are prone to conditions that require medical care. Not everyone will provide, or can afford, the time and expense required to properly care for a Shih Tzu.

More than 2,500 dogs are born every hour in the United States and more than 2.1 million dogs are euthanized (put to death humanely) annually in animal shelters. That is one dog every 15 seconds and Shih Tzus number among them. By neutering your Shih Tzu, you are helping to reduce these numbers.

Other Options

If you want to have your dog neutered but you think you may one day want a litter of puppies from him, you do have an interesting option. You can have your male's semen collected, processed, preserved, and stored by a canine sperm bank and then have your dog castrated. That way, Lotus can sire puppies even after he is castrated. When sperm is stored in liquid nitrogen, it keeps indefinitely.

Many dog breeders use frozen semen routinely in their breeding programs. Recently a large litter of Beagles was produced from frozen semen that had been stored for more than 22 years. So if you want your Shih Tzu to benefit from the health advantages of castration, but you want the security of knowing your dog can still sire puppies some time in the future—whether in the next year or in 50 years—contact a canine sperm bank.

Chapter Four

Selecting Your Shih Tzu

Where to Find a Shih Tzu

The best way to find a Shih Tzu is to begin with the American Shih Tzu Club (see Useful Literature and Web Sites, page 147) or your local Shih Tzu club. They can provide names of reputable Shih Tzu breeders. You can also join a breed, or all-breed, dog club in your area where you can meet breeders, dog trainers, and professional dog show handlers who can provide a wealth of information about various breeders.

Another source of information and possible Shih Tzu breeder contacts is through dog publications, available from your local bookstore or pet store. Dog magazines contain numerous advertisements placed by dog breeders with animals for sale. Just remember that anyone can place an advertisement and a big advertisement does not always mean the breeder is the biggest or the best. Be sure to always check out a breeder's reputation before you buy.

Word of mouth is often the best way to find a good breeder. Ask other happy Shih Tzu owners where they obtained their pet and if they are happy with its personality and health. Ask dog club members, dog groomers, dog trainers, and professional dog handlers who they would recommend. The dog world is small and the best Shih Tzu breeders are well known in canine circles.

Another good way to find just the right Shih Tzu is to attend some dog shows in your area and meet various breeders in person. Look at their animals and talk to the breeders. You will quickly determine which animals appeal to you the most and which breeders give you a sense of confidence.

Be sure to purchase from a reputable breeder. Don't be surprised if the breeder you select does not have puppies immediately available. Just remember that a good Shih Tzu is well worth the wait. If you are certain you want to be the proud owner of a Shih Tzu, it is not too early to start checking with breeders today.

Puppy or Adult?

You may choose to raise a puppy, or adopt an adolescent or adult dog. The decision depends on your personal preferences and home situation. Most people want to start with a puppy, because they want to integrate it into their family at an early age, and because puppies are so cute. But a puppy isn't a puppy for long. *Puppies are temporary beings.* In a few short months your puppy will become a dog. So if you have the opportunity to purchase a wonderful, well-mannered adolescent or adult dog, give it some serious thought. There are some distinct advantages to starting off with a more mature animal that has outgrown some of its naughty behavior attributed to "not knowing any better because he's just a puppy."

When purchasing any dog, the most important considerations are the animal's health, temperament, and personality. A dog's personality is well established by the time it is 8 to 12 weeks of age. By obtaining Lotus in a very early stage of life, you may have a positive influence on his adult personality and behavioral development. This is much easier than trying to change an established undesirable behavior in an adult dog. However, sometimes, for a variety of reasons, a breeder may have an adolescent or young adult dog available for sale. If the dog has been well socialized as a youngster and well trained, there are many advantages to purchasing an older dog. You can skip the trials and tribulations of puppyhood, including housebreaking, leash training, and basic discipline — such as training your pet not to bark, not to chew on your belongings, and not to rip up your carpet. You must be certain, however, that you and the dog are a good match. It is not unreasonable to request a brief trial period when you purchase an adult dog, so that you can be sure the animal will successfully adapt to a new family and change of lifestyle.

An older, well-trained Shih Tzu may be more expensive than a puppy. This is because the older the dog, the more time, effort, and expense the breeder has invested in it. No matter what price you pay for

You'll know the right puppy when you see it. It's the most healthy, friendly, playful one that runs up to you and seems to say, "Take me home!"

Whether you purchase a puppy or an adult, be sure to buy from a reputable Shih Tzu breeder.

your pet, just keep in mind that it will be insignificant compared to the costs you will incur in feeding, grooming supplies, toys, housing, and veterinary care during the animal's lifetime. So, *take your time, save up your money, and invest in the best.*

Selecting a Puppy

The first rule in selecting a puppy is to *take your time*. Don't rush into things and don't be an impulse buyer. It is easy to fall in love with the first (and every!) puppy you see, but don't buy the puppy because it is "cute," or because you "feel sorry for it." You risk ending up with an animal that may have serious medical or behavioral problems. Do your home-

work. Take your time and use your head before your heart. The very best way to stay on the right track and increase your chances of finding a well-socialized, well-bred, healthy Shih Tzu puppy is to buy from a reputable breeder.

Once you have located a breeder with animals available for sale, make an appointment to see the puppies in person at the breeder's convenience. Be sure to verify that they have been registered and ask for a copy of their parents' registration papers. The breeder also can provide you with a copy of the puppies' pedigree. Ask the breeder if the parents have additional certifications, for example, registration by the Canine Eye Registration Foundation (CERF), or any type of testing for freedom of inherited health problems, particularly those known to occur more frequently in the Shih Tzu breed.

Personality

Watch Lotus in his home environment at the breeder's. Is he happy and outgoing? Is he alert and active, playful and curious? Carefully observe him and his littermates for signs of good health and happy personalities. A Shih Tzu is bright, confident, outgoing, trusting, eager to investigate, and very friendly. After he has had some time to get to know you, Lotus should be affectionate and playful. *He should not be aggressive or shy*.

Physical Condition

Next, check Lotus's eyes, ears, mouth, skin, coat, and movement. The eyes should be clear and bright and the ears should be clean. Normal gums are bright pink in color.

Teeth: Make sure the dog has all his teeth. If Lotus is old enough to have lost his baby (deciduous) teeth, make sure the baby teeth have all fallen out where the adult teeth have replaced them. Sometimes the baby teeth do not come out and when the adult teeth grow in there are simply too many teeth in the mouth. Retained deciduous teeth need to be extracted! The rule is: There should never be more than one tooth of the same type in the mouth at one time. In other words, if Lotus has a baby canine tooth and an adult canine tooth, the baby tooth needs to be removed right away so that the adult teeth can grow in correctly and are

not overcrowded in the mouth. Ideally, Lotus's teeth should be in correct alignment and they should all be there. However, a missing tooth is not uncommon and is not considered a serious fault. A slightly undershot bite (the lower jaw protrudes slightly outward past the upper jaw) is normal for a Shih Tzu, although jaws that align would be the ideal. If the upper jaw protrudes over the bottom jaw, this is considered a fault. The teeth and tongue should not be visible when the mouth is closed and the lips should align properly.

Skin and coat: Check that the skin and coat are healthy and free of parasites or sores. The coat should be groomed and free of knots and mats. The importance of this cannot be overemphasized. Filth, parasites,

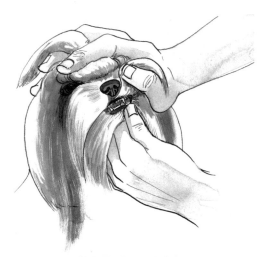

Check your Shih Tzu's teeth. It is not unusual for the bottom incisors to protrude slightly in front of the upper incisors. Your veterinarian can tell your pet's age by examining its teeth.

Littermates and Parents

Finally, ask to see Lotus's littermates and parents, if they are available. This will help you determine their personalities and give you a good idea of how you might expect Lotus to look and behave when he is an adult. Remember that the way you raise and handle Lotus, and the things he is exposed to as a youngster, will have a big influence on the way his character and temperament develop. Try to introduce him to people and different sights and sounds while he is still young and can adapt easily. The time you spend socializing Lotus as a puppy will pay off a thousand times over when he is a well-adjusted adult.

Male or Female?

If you are looking for a wonderful companion that will keep you entertained and be a faithful friend for its entire life, then either a male or female Shih Tzu will do very well. It's simply a matter of personal preference and the choice is yours.

Males and females are equally affectionate and loyal. Behavior really depends on the individual's personality and the type and amount of socialization it received as a very young puppy. With kindness, patience, and understanding, either a male or female Shih Tzu can fit nicely into the right family situation.

Size ranges from 9 to 10½ inches (22.8–26.6 cm) at the shoulders; females are usually smaller than

For those pet owners who don't want the challenges of raising a puppy, some breeders occasionally offer adolescents, adults, or retired breeders for sale.

foreign objects, and sores rapidly accumulate in tangled, matted hair. Look under the tail to be sure the area is clean and free of signs of blood or diarrhea.

Conscientious breeders are concerned about placing their puppies in caring, responsible homes. A breeder may ask you questions about your future plans for the puppy and the kind of home life the puppy will have. This is also your opportunity to ask questions, so take advantage of it.

Puppy Health Checklist

Attitude	Friendly, alert, playful, inquisitive.
Eyes	Bright, clear, free of discharge or cloudiness.
Ears	Clean, free of dirt and wax buildup; no evidence of head shaking or scratching.
Mouth	Gums bright pink; teeth and jaws properly aligned or slightly undershot; no duplicate teeth in the mouth (no retained baby teeth).
Skin and coat	Healthy, thick coat; well groomed, free of knots and mats, and with no evidence of parasites or sores.
Body condition	May seem a little plump but should not have a distended belly or thin body.
Movement	Normal gait for a puppy; may seem a bit bouncy and sometimes clumsy.

males. Height should not exceed 11 inches (28 cm) or be shorter than 8 inches (20.3 cm). Ideal weight is from 9 to 16 pounds (4–7.2 kg) and should be in proportion to the animal.

If you are thinking of raising Shih Tzus in the future, then you have to seriously consider your options and discuss these plans with the breeder, who can assist you in making an appropriate decision about which animal to purchase at the beginning. Most novice breeders begin by investing in the best female they can find, often an adult that has proven herself in the show ring as an excellent representative of the breed. She may have also previously produced a litter. Then, with the help of an experienced breeder, the novice finds the most suitable stud dog for the female and pays for his services.

When looking for a quality Shih Tzu, be patient and take your time. Invest in the best Shih Tzu you can find.

If you are not planning on breeding Shih Tzus, you definitely should have your dog, male or female, neutered as early as possible, for reasons previously discussed.

Show Dog or Cute Companion?

All Shih Tzus are, by their very nature, constant close *companions* for their owners. But not all Shih Tzus are *show dogs*. Decide if you want a top show dog for breeding and exhibiting in dog show competitions, or if you are mostly interested in a Shih Tzu as a companion and household pet. A show dog must conform to certain breed standards, such as height, conformation, and character. A companion Shih Tzu may have minor imperfections with regard to the high conformation standards of a future champion, but be wonderful in all other respects. Often the differences between a show dog and a companion dog are not readily apparent to most people. Flaws may be slight and only detected by the trained eye of a breeder or show judge, especially if they are hidden under a lot of hair. Being a companion dog only in no way diminishes a Shih Tzu's value as a loving member of the family. Although Shih Tzus have been bred for their good looks, their real purpose is to be affectionate companions for people and they definitely excel at their job. Remember, Shih Tzus were bred to be com-

Important Questions to Ask the Seller:

1. Are the pups registered with the kennel club?

2. How old are the pups and what sexes are available?

3. At what age were the pups weaned?

4. How many pups were in the litter?

5. Have the pups received any inoculations? If so, which ones?

6. Have the pups been wormed or tested for worms?

7. Have the pups had their eyes examined by a veterinary ophthalmologist? If so, ask to see the eye certification.

8. Have the pups been handled frequently and are they well socialized?

9. Have the pups received any basic training (housebreaking, leash training)?

10. What kind of food are the pups eating at this time?

11. Ask for a 48-hour health guarantee until you can have the puppy examined by your own veterinarian.

12. Ask to see the parents and littermates of the pup.

panion animals centuries before dog shows ever existed.

If you have decided that you want a show dog, be prepared to pay more for it than you would pay for a pet-quality companion. Also, keep in mind that although the parents may

Shih Tzus are not aggressive or shy and they love playmates.

be champion show dogs, there is no guarantee the puppy will turn out to be a champion, too. If you are serious about purchasing a show dog, the best advice is to buy an adult animal that already has been successful in the show ring. Even the loveliest puppy can change as it grows up and may not reach the show potential you had hoped. If you buy a puppy as a show prospect, you are guessing that the animal will attain a certain level of conformational quality after it has completed all its development and growth phases. A lot of changes can take place between puppyhood and adulthood. When you buy an adult, what you see is what you get and there is no guesswork involved.

Age and Longevity

It is a fact that small dog breeds live longer than large breeds, and the Shih Tzu is no exception. Shih Tzus are sturdy, solid little dogs and with good nutrition and loving care they may live 15 years or more. This is another reason to be particular when choosing your companion. You are making a long-term commitment!

Papers

Before making a final decision and completing the sale, be sure the puppy's health records, pedigree, and registration papers are in order. A puppy should have a health certificate signed by a veterinarian stating that the puppy has been examined and is in good health and able to leave its parents and travel. Dates of inoculations and any medications (such as worming medication) should be noted on the health certificate. Your veterinarian will need this information to set up a preventive health care program for your pet.

Bright eyes and a beautiful coat are signs of good health and nutrition.

Pedigree

One of the many pleasures of owning a purebred dog is pride of ownership and the variety of activities in which you and your companion can participate. For example, without registration papers, there is no proof of parentage or lineage. When you purchase your Shih Tzu, be sure to verify that both of his parents are registered and that he has been registered as well. Do not confuse official registration with a pedigree. A pedigree is not an official document. It is a chart showing the family tree and relatives of the puppy. It is a document prepared by the breeder, listing the dam and sire and their relatives. It does not guarantee that your dog is registered with the kennel club. Registration is an official document issued by the kennel club and is proof that your dog is purebred.

Registration

You should receive application papers from the breeder to register the puppy in your name. Once you choose a name for the puppy, complete the application form and mail it to the kennel club address on the application with the appropriate registration fee. You will then receive a certificate of registration from the kennel club listing you as the owner.

If you purchase your Shih Tzu as a young puppy born in the United States, the breeder will give you one of the following American Kennel Club (AKC) forms:

Registration application. This is a slip of blue paper that indicates the breeder, the litter registration number, the litter birth date, and the names and registration numbers of your dog's parents. There are spaces in which to write the dog's name, for the breeder to sign transfer of ownership, and for you to sign as the new owner. Some breeders require their kennel name to be included as part of the dog's name. The breeder can name the puppies before they are sold or allow the new owners to name them. Once the registration application is completed, the new owner sends it to the AKC with the appropriate fee (indicated on the application form). The new owner then receives either a full registration or a limited registration (see below).

Full Registration. This slip of white paper has a purple border and shows the registered name and number of the dog, its birth date, breed, and color. The breeder and owner are also indicated. This type of registration allows for participation in AKC competitions and events, as well as the ability to register future offspring of the animal with the AKC.

Limited Registration. This form looks exactly like a full registration certificate, except the border is orange. It provides the same documentation as a Full Registration certificate; however, puppies born from animals with Limited Registration cannot be registered with the AKC. Only the breeder, not the owner, can change an animal's status from Limited to Full Registration.

In one sense, a Limited Registration is like neutering an animal on paper. The intent is to discourage breeding that particular animal by blocking registration of its offspring. There are many reasons a breeder may choose to prevent a dog from being bred. For example, all good dog breeders do their best to not contribute to the animal overpopulation problem. In addition, a dog may have slight conformational flaws or be a nonaffected carrier of a genetic disorder that the breeder does not want to perpetuate. In some cases, the breeder simply wants to see how the dog matures and wait until it is an adult before giving it Full Registration privileges. If you are considering buying a Shih Tzu with a Limited Registration and you have any questions, be sure to ask the breeder.

Will your cute puppy grow into a beautiful adult? Ask the breeder to let you see the parents so you can get an idea of what your puppy will look like when it is fully grown.

Chapter Five

At Home with Your Shih Tzu

You have found the perfect Shih Tzu! Now you are eager to bring her home and make her feel comfortable and secure. Part of your pet's success in adapting to her new family and her new life depends on making sure you are well prepared for the new arrival. Prepare your house and yard *before* bringing the new puppy home, because once the puppy arrives, everyone will be caught up in all the excitement of the new arrival!

Your new puppy will feel more secure with a soft blanket all its own, especially if it has its mother's scent on it.

First of all, make sure your house is safe and check the yard. You might not be letting your puppy go outside in the yard just yet, but now is the perfect time to check for holes in and under the fence and to remove objects in the house and yard that can present a serious health hazard (see "Safety First," page 43).

If you have everything ready in advance and all the things on hand that the newcomer will need, the transition period will go smoothly for both of you.

Your Shih Tzu Comes Home

Dogs are creatures of habit, so any change in their daily routine or environment is potentially stressful to them in the beginning. Don't expect everything to go perfectly the first few days your new companion is home with you. Whether you bring home a puppy or an adult dog, there will be a period of adjustment for a while before your pet will feel settled in and secure.

Settling In

The "settling in" period is very important. It sets the tone for the future relationship you and your Shih Tzu will establish. The lifelong bond that you will enjoy with your pet starts from the day she comes home. As you teach your new friend about proper behavior, feeding, and sleeping arrangements, remember— patience, kindness, and consistency will be your three most valuable virtues.

Ideally, your new acquisition will have been introduced to a travel kennel before you bring her home. A travel kennel makes an ideal portable doghouse for Shih Tzus, so this is an item that you will use frequently, for travel and home. If Cookie has a favorite toy or blanket (especially a blanket that the mother has been sleeping on), ask the breeder if you can place it in the travel kennel for the trip home. A familiar item with comforting smells will help her feel more secure during the trip and during the next few days in her new environment.

Place the familiar item, or a soft blanket or towel, in the travel kennel on top of a layer of shredded newspaper. Make sure Cookie has not eaten for the last two hours so that she is less likely to become carsick and vomit. The trip home may be the first time she has ever traveled in a car. If she feels queasy, she may drool excessively, so be sure to bring along plenty of paper or terry cloth towels. Allow Cookie to relieve herself before you place her in the travel kennel.

Supplies You Will Need for Your New Shih Tzu

- Food and water dishes
- Quality puppy/dog food
- Comfortable sleeping quarters (dog bed or pillow, designated area in home)
- Travel kennel (ideal for training and for sleeping quarters)
- Identification tag
- Collar or harness
- Leash
- Grooming supplies (slicker brush, wide-toothed metal comb, blunt-tipped scissors, nail trimmers, styptic powder, gentle emollient shampoo, ear-cleaning solution)
- Dental supplies (toothbrush, dentifrice)
- First aid kit
- Exercise pen (X-pen), safety gate, or other type of safe, escape-proof enclosure
- Toys

Your new companion may protest all the way home, or she may simply sleep. Make a decision right now not to give in to her crying, no matter how difficult it is. Talk to her soothingly but be forewarned! If you hold her on your lap for the trip home, she will not forget it, and she will expect you to allow her on your lap during every car trip you take together. When she is an adult she will of course be larger and it is safer for both of you if she remains in her travel kennel whenever she travels in the car. On the other hand, if you *know* you will always be the passenger when you travel with Cookie, and that someone else will *always* be doing the driving, by all means hold her in your lap on the way home. You'll both be a lot happier and the strong bond of friendship you will share for the rest of her long life can begin to take form. When it comes to bonding, the sooner the better!

When you arrive home, give Cookie a small drink of water. Remember that she is probably fatigued from her trip and all the excitement, so a little quiet time is in order. If she is sleepy, allow her to rest. If she feels like becoming acquainted, do so calmly and gently. Avoid loud noises and sudden movements. Be sure to teach any children

When you lift your puppy, support it carefully so it is not dropped or injured.

in the home to respect Cookie's space and privacy. Teach them the proper way to lift and handle her, by gently putting one hand under her chest and the other under her hindquarters for support. *Never lift a Shih Tzu by the scruff of the neck or by the limbs.* Small children should remain seated on the floor when petting or handling a puppy, to prevent dropping or injury. It is very important that children learn from the very beginning that Cookie is a delicate, sensitive being and not a toy.

Naming Your Shih Tzu

The first thing your Shih Tzu will need to learn is her name. Once she knows her name, you can get her attention and start a line of communication—the first step in her lifelong training.

Your dog's personality will shine through from the beginning, so you will most likely have no difficulty thinking of a name that suits your companion and her character. If you need some ideas, you will find plenty in dog magazines and books of baby names.

It seems easier for dogs to recognize names with two syllables. This avoids confusion later on when you give one-syllable commands, such as *come*, *sit*, *stay*, and *down*.

When you have selected a name, use it often when talking to your new pet. When she responds or comes to you, praise her lavishly. It won't take her long to know who she is.

Housing Considerations

Your pet has lots of hair, but it won't protect her from harsh weather. Remember: *The Shih Tzu is strictly an indoor pet.* Cookie will love to play outside, but she must live indoors and she enjoys the same creature comforts you do.

When you bring Cookie home, decide on a safe place (an X-pen, laundry room, area off the kitchen) where she can feel secure and have some privacy, yet be observed. Ideally, this area will be Cookie's permanent housing and sleeping quarters. Take her to her new den to explore and relax for several minutes. Feed her a little treat and praise her. Cookie should associate her space with enjoyment. It should be a pleasant place to be. Make sure she also can observe the household activities so she doesn't feel isolated. Shih Tzus are intelligent, active dogs and they want to be in the center of everything going on around them. Exposure to various sights, sounds, smells, activities, and people are very important aspects of puppy socialization. Cookie doesn't know the rules yet and will require training, so make sure her den is in an area where she cannot chew furniture or urinate on the carpet. Later, when you have started training her, do not use her sleeping quarters as a place

When you first bring your puppy home, give it a small drink of fresh water.

to go when she is punished. Her territory should always be a comforting place where she goes when all is right with the world, and not when she is in trouble. Of course, Cookie's preferred location will always be with you or on your lap!

If you have acquired an older Shih Tzu, try to duplicate its previous housing situation as much as possible to reduce the stress of changing environments.

Safety First

Cookie will be very curious and interested in learning more about her new home. Some of the characteristics you admire most about your dog—her intelligence, small size, and activity level—also create some of the biggest problems for her safety and make her prone to accidents.

Convenient Housing Options

Travel kennels	Ideal for use as a small doghouse; lightweight, easy to clean, well ventilated; provides privacy.
Exercise pens (X-pens)	Portable, folding pens, available in a variety of sizes; attachments for dishes and water bottles.
Doghouses	Should be constructed of nonporous material; easy to clean and disinfect.
Safety gates	Useful for closing off a designated area or stairway to prevent escape or injury.
Bedding	Should be natural material (cotton, wool) because synthetic materials or bedding containing cedar shavings may cause allergies.

Believe it or not, there are countless life-threatening situations in your home. Be sure that you have removed any potential hazards before you let Cookie explore, and be sure that she is supervised at all times.

Household Cleaning Products and Chemicals

• Cleaning products and chemicals are potentially deadly for Cookie if she comes in contact with them. Some types of paints can be toxic if she chews on wooden baseboards or walls.

• Be sure to keep the seat and lid down on the toilet. You might think your Shih Tzu isn't tall enough to reach the water in the toilet, but Shih Tzus can scramble and climb into unlikely places. Many dogs like to drink from toilet bowls and a thirsty Shih Tzu might try to do that. If your pet manages to hang over the edge to drink, it's possible for her to fall inside the bowl; as strange as it sounds, it's a common accident. If you use any cleaning chemicals in the toilet tank, these can be very harmful to your pet. In the worst situations, Cookie could fall into the toilet when you are not at home and be unable to climb out. She could become very cold or even drown.

Antifreeze

Antifreeze (ethylene glycol) is a common cause of animal poisoning. This automotive chemical can be found on garage floors. It has a sweet taste and animals that drink even a very small amount will develop severe kidney damage and could die. Survival depends on an early diagnosis and immediate treatment. If you think your car is leaking antifreeze, do not allow Cookie in the garage where she might lick a small puddle or a few drops off the floor.

Note: There is now a type of antifreeze being marketed that is said to be nontoxic to animals. This product may be available in your area.

Rodent Poisons and Snap Traps

If you have any rodent bait that has been left out for wild vermin, pick it up immediately; it is as deadly for Cookie as it is for the wild rodents. If there are any dead rodents in the garage or yard that may have been poisoned, discard them. Shih Tzus are curious and investigate anything they find. If Cookie eats a poisoned animal, she can be poisoned as well.

If you have snap traps set in your house or garage, remove them. They can break small toes or injure a nose.

Electrical Shock

Electrocution from gnawing on an electrical cord is a real potential danger that could cost Cookie her life and possibly cause an electrical fire. Keep her away from them!

Kitchen and Appliances

When pets get underfoot, accidents happen. They can be burned from hot liquids that have spilled from pots on the stove, or from a hot iron falling on them from the ironing board after a tangle in the electrical cord. Before you do the laundry, check the dryer. Incredibly, many small pets have been found, too late, inside the dryer, where they had settled in for a cozy snooze.

Doors and Windows

Make sure all doors to the outside or to the garage are securely closed.

When you can't be with your puppy, keep it in a secure area with an easy-to-clean floor. Be sure to give your puppy some toys to prevent boredom.

Shih Tzus love to sit up on furniture and look out the window. Your windows and screens should be securely fastened so that Cookie

Make sure the yard and garden are safe for your puppy. Remove chemicals such as fertilizers, rodent bait, and insecticides and check for holes in the fence.

Shih Tzus love to look out windows. Make sure they are securely fastened so your pet doesn't fall out the window.

cannot fall out of the window and be injured. If Cookie escapes outdoors, she can become lost or may be the victim of an automobile accident. To prevent a broken tail or toes, be certain Cookie is not in the way when you close doors.

Injuries from Humans

Everyone in the house must pay close attention to where they step. Shih Tzus are small, always close by, and move quickly. Cookie can be underfoot before you know it and be stepped on and hurt. If you try to sidestep her, you also can be injured if you lose your balance, trip, or fall.

Poisonous Plants

Many ornamental plants are toxic to animals, including philodendron, dieffenbachia, foxglove, and lily of the valley. Keep household plants out of reach and limit home and gar-den plants to nontoxic varieties. If you have any doubt about whether a plant is toxic, check with the grower or nursery before you purchase the plant.

Foreign Objects

Dogs explore with their mouths and often will eat anything, even if it doesn't taste very good. Make sure that small balls, children's toys, rubber bands, paper clips, pens, sewing needles, and anything else you can think of are out of your pet's reach. Coins are a special hazard because pennies contain high levels of zinc and can cause zinc poisoning. Be sure that any toys you purchase are safe and do not contain small pieces, bells, or whistles that may present a choking hazard.

Garbage

As unappealing as it may seem to us, most dogs insist on exploring garbage cans. In addition to the obvious hazards associated with this activity, dogs may also suffer from "garbage poisoning," a form of poisoning caused by bacteria and bacterial toxins found in old and decaying foods.

Candies and Medicines

Make sure you have not left any foods or medicine containers within your dog's reach. An overdose of common medicines including aspirin, acetaminophen (Tylenol), ibuprofen (Advil, Motrin), and naproxen (Aleve) can be fatal for her. Chocolate contains a methylxanthine substance, similar to caffeine, called theobromine that is toxic to dogs. Hard candies can become lodged between the teeth at the back of the jaw or in the throat and become a serious choking hazard.

Holidays are when most dogs run into trouble because owners leave goodies out on the coffee table for all of the family to share. Unfortunately, your little "under the table" dog is not so small that she can't reach on top of the coffee table and she will not hesitate to help herself to as much as she wants.

Identification

The very first thing you should do once you have brought your new companion home is to be sure she is properly identified. If Cookie ever becomes lost, your chances of being reunited are very slim without proper identification. Ninety percent of all lost family pets are unidentifiable, and 70 percent of these animals never return home. Annually, millions of lost American pets are euthanized. Don't let Cookie become one of the statistics. If she doesn't yet have identification, stop whatever you are doing and have her identified *right now*. You'll be glad you did.

Microchips

One of the most effective forms of animal identification is a microchip. A microchip is a microtransponder the size of a grain of rice that is implanted under the skin quickly and easily by injection. The microchip has

a series of numbers unique to itself so that each animal has its own identification number. A handheld scanner (also called a decoder or reader) is used to read the identification number. Microchips are safe, permanent, and tamper-proof. The entire identification procedure (microchip implant or scanning) takes only a few seconds. Scanning is absolutely painless and accurate.

Once an animal has been implanted with a microchip, the following information is entered into a central computer registry: animal's identification number, a description of the animal, the owner's name, address, and telephone number, and an alternate contact in case the owner cannot be reached. It is the owner's responsibility to update the registry in the event of a change in

Buy only safe toys for your Shih Tzu. Some chew toys, including rawhide bones, can break off in pieces and become lodged in your pet's throat, causing choking, suffocation, and death.

A collar with a nametag is an excellent form of identification. Do not put a collar on a tiny puppy. Check the collar often as your Shih Tzu grows to make sure it is not too tight.

information. An identification tag for the animal's collar also is provided, indicating the animal's identification number and the registry's telephone number.

Lost animals can be identified at animal shelters, humane societies, and veterinary offices. Once the animal's identification number is displayed, the central registry is contacted and the owner's information is released.

Surprisingly, the cost for all of this technology, including the microchip and its implantation, is modest. At the time of this writing, it is approximately $40. In addition, the price for lifetime enrollment in the American Kennel Club Animal Recovery data-

base is currently only $12.50. For the life of your pet, this is an investment you cannot afford to deny it.

Collars and Nametags

Collars and nametags are an excellent form of identification. Besides, every dog needs a collar or harness and a leash. These are the essential pieces of equipment for training and restraining your pet.

If your dog wears a wide, flat, nylon collar or harness when you take it for walks, you can write your name and phone number on it. If a light nylon or leather collar is used, you can have a nametag engraved to attach to it. Many local pet stores offer on-the-spot nametag engraving. Collars and tags are easily visible and let others know your lost companion has a family.

Note: *Slip or choke collars are inappropriate for Shih Tzus unless they have been trained to this type of collar. Never leave your pet unattended wearing a slip or choke collar. They can accidentally catch or hang on objects and your Shih Tzu could strangle to death.*

Tattoos

Tattoos are considered a good form of identification because they are visible and permanent. Most veterinarians offer tattoo identification for dogs. Shih Tzus may be tattooed on the ear flap, inner thigh, or belly. Tattoos prove legal, unquestionable ownership and discourage potential theft by would-be dognappers. However, if you decide to have Cookie tattooed, do not rely entirely on this method to help find her if she is ever lost. Be sure to keep your address and telephone number current with the tattoo registry(ies) you select.

Some clinics, humane societies, and animal shelters use a tattoo, usually a simple "S," to indicate if a female is spayed.

A tattoo of any kind is a visible way to say an animal has an owner. Some animal shelters will give a tattooed animal a grace period of a few additional days of housing before euthanizing it. Just the fact that a tattoo could buy your pet precious time if it ever found itself in such a sad situation makes a tattoo valuable.

Identification Is Important!

The best thing you can do to increase the chances for a safe return of your lost, injured, or stolen pet is give her as many forms of identification as possible.

1. All dogs should have a collar or harness and an identification tag.

2. All dogs should be microchipped and registered with the microchip registry.

3. All dogs should be registered with the American Kennel Club Animal Recovery Database.

4. Have your Shih Tzu tattooed.

The cost of animal identification is nothing compared to the tragedy of losing your canine friend. What price would you have to pay if your pet were lost? Advertising fees for newspaper ads in the Lost and Found columns, fees to make posters, time to post the notices, long-distance phone calls, and time to search the neighborhood and visit the animal shelter every day are just a few of the costs you would incur. You might also have a reward fee to pay in the unlikely event you were lucky enough to have your pet returned safely home to you. And then there are all the tears and sleepless nights as you worry about where your dog is and whether she is all right. By comparison, the modest cost of identification is nothing at all. So, protect your pet and save yourself a lot of heartache. *Identify your Shih Tzu today!*

House-training Your Shih Tzu

House-training your Shih Tzu may be a challenge, but you'll get it done. What's the secret? Patience, diligence, consistency, making sure your puppy gets to the right place at the right time, and lots of praise.

Shih Tzus are meticulous about their living quarters and will do their best not to soil where they are housed or confined. This is another excellent reason for keeping Cookie in a travel kennel on the way home from the breeder's. If the trip was not too long, she probably will have waited to urinate or defecate.

• You can start out right by taking her outside immediately upon arrival and placing her where you want her

When you have to be away, or during the night, confine your puppy to an area and cover the floor with newspapers. Your puppy will use the papers for its toilet until it is completely housebroken.

to learn to do her business. She will immediately urinate, and when she does, praise her repeatedly. You are off to a positive start.

• Next, place Cookie in her designated living area. This area should have easy-to-clean flooring, such as tile or linoleum, but no carpeting. Remember that she has a very small bladder and does not yet have full control of bladder or bowels. She will need to go outside frequently and certainly will have a few accidents before she is fully trained. But remember also that Cookie wants to please. As soon as she understands that she should urinate or defecate only in the area you have indicated, she will try her best to wait until you take her to that spot. If she soils in her confinement, it is an accident, so don't punish her. The outdated and cruel training methods of rubbing a dog's nose in its urine, or hitting a dog, are the worst things you can do.

• Don't raise your voice or reprimand Cookie. She will not associate your scolding with her natural body functions, especially if the scolding occurs long after the act of elimination.

Scolding

Be reasonable. If you scold your puppy too harshly, she may become confused and behave just the opposite of the way you would like her to behave. She may become less sociable, or withdraw from you. Everything is new and strange to her, and like a baby, she has little control over her elimination at this point. Rather, clean up the mess and work

Shih Tzus are very sensitive. Do not scold your puppy harshly. It will become unhappy and less sociable, and will withdraw from you.

on positive reinforcement by praising her profusely when she does the right thing. Without recognition and praise for good behavior, Shih Tzus can become stubborn and uncooperative. Remember, it's difficult, if not impossible, to make a Shih Tzu do something it doesn't want to do—it's up to you to make house-training fun and rewarding so Cookie wants to participate and please you.

Watch for Signs

Cookie doesn't know how to tell you when she needs to go. For now, it is up to you to be attentive to her needs and signs of impending urination or defecation so you can take her outside in time. Signs include sniffing the ground, pacing, circling, whining, crying, and acting anxious.

You must act fast as soon as this behavior begins or you will be too late! Cookie will always need to urinate immediately after waking up from a nap or after eating a meal, so in these instances, take her directly outside without waiting for signs. Remember to lavish praise on her for her performance.

Schedules

One of the keys to successful house-training is to set up a regular schedule to let Cookie out to do her business. Ideally, a young puppy should be let outside every few hours. Of course, there will be times when you simply cannot be available to do this. When you have to be away from the house for long periods of time, keep Cookie restricted to a designated, confined area and cover the floor of the area with newspapers. She will do her best to urinate and defecate on the papers. Now she has the right idea and is learning to control her elimination until she reaches a given spot, even if it isn't yet the backyard.

The Kennel Crate

The kennel crate is an ideal house-training tool. Keep Cookie confined in the kennel, with plenty of bedding, overnight. She will do her best not to soil her sleeping quarters. Just be sure to get up early to let her outside. It's unfair for you to sleep in while you make your puppy wait for a long time with a full bladder!

You may have been told that if your puppy soils her kennel crate, you should leave her confined in the crate for an additional 30 minutes, along with her excrement. *This is not good advice!* The idea is that this will be so unpleasant for your puppy that she will learn more quickly to hold herself until she can go outside. The truth is, it will be miserable for your Shih Tzu to be confined with her

How Often Is Often Enough?

Puppies should be let outside to urinate, or placed on newspaper in a designated area, at least every three hours. If your puppy has just eaten, there is more pressure on the bladder and it should be placed in its "toilet area" immediately to prevent an accident.

In Case of an Accident on the Carpet

There are several carpet cleaning products designed specifically for removal of pet odors and stains. Some of these are available from your veterinarian or your local pet supply stores. However, if you don't have any of these commercial products immediately available, and if your puppy accidentally soils the carpet, here are two simple solutions that may help. You may try one or the other, but be sure to test a small section of your carpet first, to be sure the solution does not damage it:
• Mix one part clear vinegar to one part water and lightly dab or blot on carpet with a clean towel.
• Take a small amount of club soda and dab it lightly on the carpet and blot it dry with a clean towel.

solid waste material, but it will be much worse for you! Never mind the odor—you will also have a bigger mess to clean up than you would have had in the first place, because your puppy might step in her feces or accidentally lie in the mess and get everything in her hair. Then you will have more than the crate to clean; you will have to groom your puppy from head to tail. This is a poor training technique that is not usually successful. It just makes extra work for you. Shih Tzus try hard not to soil their houses, dens, or sleeping areas. If your pet has had

The Courteous Cleanup Crew—*You!*

• When you take your pet outside, don't forget the essentials! Take a plastic bag or a "pooper scooper" to promptly pick up the mess and discard it properly in a well-sealed plastic bag. Don't bury the excrement in the ground where it can be stepped on or other animals can find it.

• Dog feces may contain contagious organisms that can spread diseases (such as parvovirus or intestinal parasites). Some of these are contagious to other dogs and some are contagious to people (such as roundworms, which can be a serious problem for children).

• Be thoughtful and courteous to others. Keep your environment pristine and safe for people and animals to enjoy.

Puppies need to be let outside frequently. As your puppy learns house manners, it may act anxious or try to get your attention when it needs to go outside.

an accident, it's probably because she had to wait longer than she was capable of waiting. The easiest solution is to take your puppy outside at more frequent intervals.

When Cookie is a little older, you can restrict her to her kennel crate for brief periods of time when you have to be away. Since Shih Tzus will not soil their "den," when you return, be sure to take Cookie outside immediately. Don't use the kennel crate for house-training, however, if you have to be away for extended periods of time. Cookie needs space to be comfortable. She needs to be able to get up and run around and if she's in her kennel crate for too long it will become more like a prison to her than a safe den.

Note: If your Shih Tzu (puppy or adult) is house-trained and starts having accidents in the house, this could be a sign of medical problems such as a bladder infection. Consult your veterinarian.

Outside

When you take Cookie out to relieve herself, stay and wait with her. If you go into the house she may become distracted and worried and try to find you. She may forget why she has been let outside because she is too concerned about where you are. And if you are in the house, you won't know for sure if Cookie did

House-training Tips

1. Start house-training your Shih Tzu the day she arrives—it is never too early!

2. Make sure your puppy is receiving good nutrition, has normal stools, and is free of internal parasites.

3. Keep your Shih Tzu on a regular feeding schedule and don't feed her table scraps or treats during the training period.

4. Let your puppy outside several times a day, first thing in the morning, after every meal, after naps, and as late as possible in the evening.

5. Never scold your puppy if she has an accident.

6. Praise her profusely when she does the right thing.

7. Learn to recognize the signs that your puppy needs to go outside.

8. Be patient and be understanding.

anything outside. You may bring her inside before she has finished and she could have an accident in the house shortly afterward. That's a preventable setback in the training program.

It's also good to check on how your puppy urinates and defecates. If your Shih Tzu is having trouble eliminating, or if she has diarrhea or worms, you may not notice unless you are in the yard when she is and you see what she does. (In those cases, collecting a fresh stool specimen to take to your veterinarian for diagnosis is an important step in your puppy's health care.)

Waiting

Eventually, Cookie will be able to wait for longer periods of time as she develops more bowel and bladder control. It will be a while before she can wait until morning to urinate, but during that time she will use the newspapers you leave on the floor.

House-training is the result of two-way communication. You teach Cookie that she must eliminate outside, and she must find a way to let you know her desire to go outside when nature calls. She may never "ask" to go outside by barking or scratching at the door or fetching her leash like the dogs in the movies. But if she hasn't been outside for a long period of time, or just woke up, or finished a meal, or acts anxious or apprehensive and starts to pant and stare at you, you know what to do.

Exercise

Exercise is an important part of all Shih Tzus' physical and mental health. Shih Tzus are by nature busy, active, inquisitive dogs. They enjoy interesting outings and if left alone for long periods of time, they bore easily, become depressed, or get into mischief.

Your Shih Tzu does not need a large backyard to keep in shape. What she really needs is for you to develop a healthy exercise program suitable for her age, stage of development, health, and physical abilities. Cookie should have regular play sessions and walks every day. She depends on you to make it happen because she certainly will not exercise sufficiently on her own. She just might, however, chew up the furniture if she has nothing else to do, so keep her busy!

When you begin to plan Cookie's exercise program, remember that all animals must first build up endurance gradually. This requires a regular routine that, over time, may increase in length or vigor. Whatever you do, do not take Cookie out for infrequent, strenuous exercise. After all, Shih Tzus were bred to be close companions, following in your footsteps but not overexerting. There is a limit to what Shih Tzus can do physically, because of their physical build and the size and shape of their nasal passages. But this doesn't mean that a Shih Tzu is fragile. Shih Tzus are sturdy. But like all dogs (and people!), Cookie must start with a moderate exercise program and build it up gradually to a level suitable for her age and health condition.

A regular exercise program will improve Cookie's cardiovascular endurance and function, build strong bones and joints, and develop muscles and muscle tone. Before you start her on an exercise program, have her examined by your veterinarian and ask for exercise activity recommendations tailored to her needs and abilities.

Exercise Activities for Your Shih Tzu

Walking

Walking is a good form of exercise. It is also strenuous, so start with short walks each day and very gradually increase the distance. Cookie's natural pace is different from your own and she has to take a lot of steps to equal one of your strides, so don't hesitate to slow down to accommodate her. Watch Cookie closely for signs of tiring and stop if she becomes tired. If she overexerts, she can become sore or develop muscle spasms and lameness.

Surfaces: Whenever possible, let Cookie exercise on soft surfaces, such as lawns or sandy beaches. Sidewalks and asphalt are hot, uncomfortable, and hard on the joints upon impact. Rocky or gravel

Shih Tzus love to run and play. Daily exercise, on soft surfaces, will keep your pet healthy.

Hot Surfaces Hurt!

- Make sure the sidewalk, sand, or asphalt is not hot when you take your pet on a walk. If the ground is hot to the touch and too uncomfortable to stand on in your bare feet, it's painful for your Shih Tzu as well.
- Remember that your companion is short and her belly is near the ground. Heat radiates upward. Black surfaces can be especially hot. Little footpads burn quickly and hot surfaces can quickly overheat your pet.
- Pay close attention to where your dog walks. Make sure the ground temperature is not hot so you can *both* enjoy your walks. If the ground becomes too hot, carry your Shih Tzu so she will not have to suffer.

A walk in the snow can be invigorating, but don't let your Shih Tzu get too cold. When you get home, rinse any rock salt from your pet's feet and dry the coat thoroughly.

surfaces are also hard on your pet's small feet. Be sure to check Cookie's feet for stickers, torn toenails, cuts, or abrasions at the end of every walk. If she develops foot sores, treat them and discontinue the walks until the lesions have completely healed. If you live in an area with snow, don't walk Cookie on salted roadways and be sure to rinse her feet after each walk so she doesn't develop salt burns. Finally, try to work on level surfaces, especially if Cookie is young and still in her developmental growth phase, or if she is older, or suffering from arthritis. Climbing hills and stairs can be very hard on growing bones and joints or aged hips and joints, especially for a small dog with short limbs. Keep Cookie's needs and limitations well in mind. Exercise should be fun and beneficial for her. It should not be stressful or cause injury or pain.

Swimming

Swimming is a good form of exercise—for some dogs. It builds stamina and works most of the muscles in the body. Swimming is particularly good for older animals because it allows for exercise without impact or trauma to aged joints and bones. But not all Shih Tzus enjoy the water and the Shih Tzu's coat was not designed to be in and out of chlorinated pool water that can damage a beautiful coat. Many brachycephalic (flat-faced, short-nosed) breeds have trouble in the water because it is hard to breathe through small nasal passages and swim at the same time. Nevertheless, if Cookie likes to swim, a few minutes now and then can be fun.

Never leave your Shih Tzu unattended in the water. If she swims in a pool, be certain she knows where the stairs are and train her how to get out of the pool, but never leave her alone. Be sure Cookie does not become overly tired or chilled. Rinse out any chlorine or salt water from her hair, dry her thoroughly, and

Swimming is good exercise for some dogs, but strenuous for a Shih Tzu because its brachycephalic face makes breathing while swimming difficult. Supervise your pet when it plays in or near water.

Tea Solution for Tender Feet

Here is a formula that you can mix and *apply* to your Shih Tzu's feet to help toughen foot pads and dry sore lesions. *Do not allow your pet to drink this solution!*

1. Boil 2 cups of water.

2. Steep 10 orange pekoe black teabags in the water for 20 minutes.

3. Crush 10 aspirin tablets (325 mg tablets) and dissolve them in the tea solution.

4. Allow the mixture to cool before using.

5. Apply solution to affected areas of the footpads three to four times daily until lesions are healed. (If the lesions are raw or open, do not add aspirin to the solution.)

This solution will keep for several months when stored in a tightly closed jar.

Never leave your Shih Tzu unattended in or near water. If you have a pool, pond, or spa, place an emergency ramp in it. Train your Shih Tzu how to use the ramp to climb out of the water in case it accidentally falls in when you are not there.

Exercise Reminders
- Always keep your Shih Tzu on a leash when you are exercising her in public. This act of responsible dog ownership will greatly reduce the chances of loss or injury.
- Be sensitive to your dog's needs. If she is panting excessively and having difficulty keeping up, stop exercising immediately! She may be suffering from overexertion or heatstroke. Remember, in order to keep up with you, she has to take several rapid steps for every one of your own.

comb her out very well after each swim. Make sure her eyes are not irritated and her ears are completely dried. Although swimming may be fun once in a while for your Shih Tzu, it may be more work for you than you want to do. If that's the case, keep your canine away from the water!

Fetch
Many Shih Tzus will retrieve objects for their owners, although they are not always willing to immediately give them back! You can use a wide variety of interesting objects for this game, including balls, dumbbells, and soft stuffed toys.

Tracking
Shih Tzus have a good sense of smell. If you want to make an interesting game for Cookie, try hiding little tidbits around the house or yard for her to find. You can make the game more complicated by hiding the treats one to two hours in advance of the search and increasing the distance between treats. The advantages to this type of exercise are that they encourage your pet to be active, increase her tracking ability, and you can set the course at your leisure. If Cookie seems to have a natural ability for this game, consider contacting the American Kennel Club for a Tracking Regulations brochure. Cookie may be gifted. Whether she's a candidate for earning a Tracking Dog title or not, she will surely love your tracking games at home.

Toys

Shih Tzus love interesting toys and all toys seem to end up as chew toys, whether designed for that purpose or not. With this in mind, you should always be sure that the toys you buy are durable and safe.

Chew toys can enrich Cookie's life by providing stimulation of the gums and exercise of the jaws, as well as helping to pass the time and avoid boredom when you are not home. Some chew toys help reduce tartar buildup on the teeth. Chew toys are useful tools to help keep Cookie from chewing on valuables, such as furniture or clothing. Never give Cookie an old shoe or piece of clothing as a chew toy. She will not know the difference between an old, discarded item and your most expensive clothing or shoes. By allowing Cookie to chew on old shoes, you tell her that anything in your closet is fair game. Don't confuse her!

Not all toys are suitable for Shih Tzus; for example, cow hooves, available as chew toys in local pet stores, are very hard and may actually cause a tooth to fracture. Large

Safe toys are chew-proof and durable. Toys that shred, tear, or break into small pieces can get caught in your pet's throat or intestines.

rawhide knots and twists are dangerous because they can be swallowed and obstruct or block the gastrointestinal tract. (Small rawhide chew sticks are generally softer and may be acceptable chew toys.) Other toys may break, shred, or tear and become lodged in the airway passages or gastrointestinal tract. Small metal squeakers from soft latex toys, or little button eyes of dolls,

Dangerous Toys	Risks
Rawhide formed into bone shapes	"Knots" of rawhide or other shapes can obstruct the trachea
Latex toys, rubber toys, cotton ropes, hard plastic toys	May shred or break and obstruct the gastrointestinal tract
Toys small enough to be swallowed	May obstruct trachea or gastrointestinal tract

You can never have too many toys. It's no fun if someone doesn't want to share!

sometimes fall out when they are chewed on and can be inhaled or block the trachea and cause choking or suffocation.

The best toys are those that cannot break or shred, are too big to be swallowed, and can also provide dental prophylaxis (gum stimulation and removing tartar buildup on the teeth).

The toys you buy Cookie will depend on the kind of dog she is. Some Shih Tzus are very gentle with their toys and would never try to tear them apart. Other Shih Tzus are interested in finding out what's inside every toy they own!

Traveling Can Be Fun

Shih Tzus love to travel and a well-mannered Shih Tzu makes a wonderful ambassador for the breed. Whether you are on a long vacation, or a short outing, the company and companionship of your Shih Tzu can make the trip all the more fun.

1. Make sure Cookie is trained to her travel kennel and feels comfortable and secure inside of it. This training begins early in life, by using the travel crate daily as a security den and placing food tidbits in it periodically. When it comes time to take a trip, she will feel at home in her travel kennel and will not be stressed or fret.

2. Obtain a health certificate for travel.

• Make sure Cookie is in excellent health and able to make the trip.

• Ask your veterinarian to do a physical examination and verify that all necessary vaccinations are up to date.

• Ask if any special medications for the trip are recommended (for example, medication for the prevention of heartworm in certain states, or medication for carsickness).

3. Make sure you have all the things you will need during the trip, including items in case of illness or emergency:
• Travel kennel
• Collar with identification tag and leash
• Dishes, food, and bottled water
• Medications
• First aid kit
• Toys and bedding from home
• Grooming supplies
• Cleanup equipment: pooper scooper, plastic bags, and paper towels.
• Veterinary records, photo identification, microchip number, and contact phone numbers
    4. Make reservations in advance.
• Check with hotels or campgrounds to be sure pets are permitted.
• Reserve space for a dog with the airlines if air travel is part of your travel plans.

Traveling by Air

If you are traveling by air and Cookie is accustomed to her travel kennel, tranquilizers are seldom necessary for air travel, are sometimes ineffective, and are often discouraged as tranquilization might hinder breathing if your pet is heavily sedated.

Cookie may be small enough to fit comfortably under the seat in front of you in her travel crate. If she is not, she will be assigned a space in the cargo hold. Be sure to make advance

Kennel crates are ideal for travel. They are also useful for house-training and serve as a safe den. Don't leave your Shih Tzu confined for long periods of time.

Travel Tips
    1. Train your Shih Tzu to a travel kennel.
    2. Make a few short practice trips, even if it's just driving around the block.
    3. Obtain a health certificate for out-of-state travel.
    4. Make reservations well in advance and advise hotels and airlines you are traveling with a pet.
    5. Allow your pet to have a drink of *bottled* water every few hours to prevent dehydration.
    6. If you are visiting friends, be courteous and make sure they don't mind if you bring your dog. Not everyone loves dogs as much as you do!
    7. Make a list of everything you will need and pack well in advance.

reservations. With heightened airline security, not all airlines are currently shipping animals in cargo, so check with the airlines before you make reservations. Also, ask the airline company what their specific requirements are so that you will be prepared *before* you arrive at the airport.

Only a limited number of animals may travel on a given flight, either in the cabin or in the cargo hold, so make your reservation as early as you can. The cargo hold is temperature controlled and pressurized just like the cabin in which you travel. Don't worry about your traveling companion; she will probably sleep better on the plane than you will!

Traveling by Car

If your plans include travel by car, remember that some dogs have a tendency to become carsick. To reduce the likelihood that Cookie will be carsick, limit her food and water three hours before the trip begins and, if possible, place her crate where she can see outside of the car. Although dogs become carsick from anxiety about travel, tranquilizers are not always effective in preventing carsickness. Another option you may wish to discuss with your veterinarian is the use of an antihistamine (Antivert, meclizine) that has been shown to be effective for some dogs.

Most important: *Remember to never leave your Shih Tzu in a parked car on a hot day, even for a few minutes*. Your Shih Tzu cannot tolerate hot weather and will have difficulty breathing because of the physical structure of her face and nasal passages. The temperature inside a car, even with the windows cracked open and parked in the shade, can soar past 120°F (49°C) within a few short minutes and your pet can rapidly die of heatstroke.

Children and Shih Tzus

Approaching the Shih Tzu

The Shih Tzu's appeal spans all age ranges. Children are drawn to the Shih Tzu for its endearing appearance and small size, but children must be taught to respect these dignified, proud dogs and to resist the temptation to touch until the dog

Never leave any pet in a car unattended on a warm day, even with the windows partially open. Temperatures rise rapidly and your Shih Tzu could quickly die of heatstroke.

has had time to become acquainted. The Shih Tzu is a friendly, trusting, affectionate dog. It should not be mishandled. Teach children to approach Cookie gently and to pet her only with permission and under your supervision. Shih Tzus are sweet, gentle, and mild mannered, but under the wrong circumstances, accidents can happen.

Children should learn to not put their face up close against an animal. It is very tempting to rub a cheek across the soft fur, or even to try to kiss the pet, but this should be discouraged. Because young children are short and their heads are large in proportion to their bodies, the majority of all animal bite wounds inflicted on children (regardless of animal species) happen in the area of the face and head.

Petting and Handling

The next thing children should learn is how to properly pet and handle their new canine companion. Demonstrate the correct way to lift the puppy, by placing one hand under its hindquarters and the other hand under its chest and abdomen for support. Many children are too small or have hands too small to hold a puppy or an adolescent Shih Tzu. Under adult supervision, however a child can sit on the floor and hold the puppy in his or her lap. Teach children not to lift your Shih Tzu by its legs. Your pet could be dropped or its limbs could be injured, dislocated, or broken. Also, don't try to lift your Shih Tzu by the nape of the neck

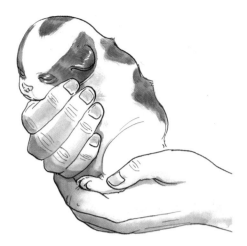

Tiny Shih Tzu puppies should be handled very carefully, using both hands.

(skin on the back of the neck). This is uncomfortable for a Shih Tzu. It will struggle and try to get away and may be dropped and injured. It may also cause the animal's eyes to bulge. In some cases, if the skin is pulled back too tightly, especially around the head, one or both eyes can proptose (be forced out from their sockets and require immediate veterinary care to save the eye and vision). For a Shih Tzu, the "scruff of the neck restraint technique" is a definite "no-no." It is dangerous and painful.

Learning from the Shih Tzu

With adult guidance, there is no limit to the things children can learn from a Shih Tzu. These wonderful dogs provide an excellent opportunity for adults to teach children about pets, the importance of humane care and treatment, kindness, and respect for life. They provide a way for very

63

Children and Shih Tzus can form wonderful friendships. With adult guidance, children can learn how to properly handle and care for their canine companion.

young children to learn responsibility by participating in the animal's care, learning the importance of providing fresh water, good food, a clean home, and a kind heart. Older children can learn a lot about animal behavior, training, exhibiting, and grooming. A Shih Tzu can be not only a dear friend to a child, it can serve as a confidant and a subordinate, something children rarely find. For a growing child, these are precious gifts that help develop confidence and character.

Some children are frightened or uncomfortable around dogs, especially large ones. Because a Shih Tzu is small and appealing, it can be possible for a child to replace anxiety, fear, or timidity with tenderness and affection. Adult supervision is necessary when a child is caressing any dog of any breed.

Even children who are somewhat shy will often talk freely when they are in the presence of animals. The Shih Tzu has historically served as a gift of friendship, opening doors of communication between rulers and dignitaries. It makes sense that your Shih Tzu will also be a noble ambassador in your household, opening doors of communication and learning for a child. While watching a Shih Tzu at play, or taking it on a walk, a child becomes a captive audience and a good learner. Together you and a child can share thoughts and ideas about animals, people, families, and anything else you can relate to Shih Tzus and humans on the child's level.

Animal Life and Death

The most difficult thing about owning and loving a pet is the knowledge that even with the very best of care, old age or illness, and eventually death, cannot be avoided. Because Shih Tzus have a relatively long life span compared to other kinds of pets, you and your family will have developed a long friendship and a deep attachment to this canine family member over the years. Children are very sensitive to issues of animal life and death, and the death of a family pet may be the first loss a child experiences. When the time comes to say good-bye to a long-time companion, children are as grief-stricken, if not more so, as adults.

It is very important that the child is prepared in advance for the eventual, and inevitable, loss or death of a beloved pet. It is especially important that this preparation be provided in a compassionate manner appropriate for the child's age and level of maturity. The loss of a pet is a very emotional experience for a child, but if handled skillfully, this loss can be turned into a positive learning experience. It provides an opportunity in which you may openly discuss life, love, illness, or death and possibly address additional fears or concerns the child may have. The sadness from the loss of one special Shih Tzu will be outweighed by the important role it played as a family member helping a child grow, mature, and strengthen in character.

Your Shih Tzu will be a treasured family member for many years.

Chapter Six

Grooming Your Shih Tzu

One of the greatest joys of owning a Shih Tzu is showing it off at its best. Wherever you go with your little "lion dog," he will encounter lots of admirers that are as captivated by his charm as you are. Because Lotus is so friendly and attractive, people will find it hard to resist an invitation to caress his soft coat. Of course, Lotus

Whether in the show ring or in the garden, a beautiful Shih Tzu is always the center of attention. Daily grooming will keep your little "lion dog" looking its best.

will love the attention. Whether you are preparing for the show ring or for a walk in the park, daily grooming will keep your pet's coat and skin in top condition and is a very important part of his health care program.

Be forewarned! Shih Tzus require *a lot* of grooming and hair care. The stunning, profuse, flowing coat for which the Shih Tzu is recognized is not created overnight. It is the result of daily brushing and combing to keep the skin healthy and the coat clean and free of mats and tangles.

Genetics, Health, and Good Care

A beautiful coat is also the product of inheritance. Coat quality, density, length, texture, and color are inherited from the parents. If your Shih Tzu does not have the genetics necessary to grow a wonderful show coat, then all the products in the world (shampoos, rinses, nutritional supplements, brushes, and combs) won't produce a quality show coat worthy of a champion. This doesn't mean your pet won't benefit from special hair care and products to help it look its very best. It simply means you must be realistic in your expectations. It's important to understand from the beginning that there are no substitutes for good genetics that can be purchased at the pet store. A beautiful show coat starts when you purchase a healthy, quality Shih Tzu puppy with excellent ancestry from a reputable breeder.

In the same way, a Shih Tzu with the genetic potential to grow a gorgeous coat will not be able to do so unless it is in excellent health, receives the best of care and nutritious food, and the environmental conditions are just right. For example, quality and balanced nutrition, clean comfortable housing, daily grooming, and regular exercise are absolutely necessary in order for your companion to grow a coat to its full potential. Many skin and hair problems are caused by poor or inadequate nutrition, food allergies, parasites (internal and external), fungi, harsh chemicals or inappropriate products used on the skin, or allergies to synthetic bedding material. Dry skin can result from a hot, dry environment. It is not uncommon to see Shih Tzus with dry flaky skin during the winter when they are exposed to the drying effects of heaters, radiators, and fireplaces. An unsanitary or damp environment can cause skin problems such as bacterial and fungal infections or parasitic infestations.

Most dogs housed outdoors grow coats that help them adapt to the seasons. Coats shed in the summer and grow thicker in the winter. Shih Tzus are *indoor* dogs that should *not* be housed outside. A refreshing outing is always welcome exercise, but Shih Tzus should live indoors. The elegant Shih Tzu was bred and raised as a house pet for centuries, from the time it graced the palace courts in Asia to now, as it embellishes your living room and enriches your life. Although Shih Tzus are sturdy, hardy animals, they were never intended to tolerate harsh weather conditions, heat, or extremes in temperature. So keep your Shih Tzu indoors where he can stay clean and comfortable. Give Lotus the pampering he deserves!

Be gentle in those tender, hard to groom areas. Make grooming a pleasant, relaxing experience for your Shih Tzu. Praise and reward your pet after grooming sessions.

Hair Growth

Your Shih Tzu's hair does not grow continuously. Hair grows in cycles. The active growth cycle is called the anagen phase. The catagen phase is a transitional period leading to the resting phase, when hair is retained in the hair follicle as dead hair, called the telogen phase. The important role quality nutrition and state of health play in hair growth cannot be overemphasized. Hair is made up of almost solid protein, called keratin. A balanced diet containing quality, digestible protein is essential for growing a beautiful coat. Although a single dog hair in the ana-

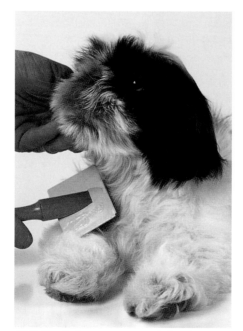

Shih Tzu haircare starts early in life. Beautiful hair is a result of inheritance (genetics), excellent health and nutrition, and regular grooming.

gen phase may grow only .1 to .2 mm each day, if you multiply that distance times the hundreds of thousands of growing hairs on your pet's body, that totals more than 50 feet (150 m) of hair growth each day! If your Shih Tzu receives a poor diet or is not in excellent health, hair growth can be shortened, delayed, or halted. Parts of the hair, such as the cuticles, can be faulty and the hair will be dull and lackluster. Hormonal imbalances can also cause hair loss or skin problems. Hormonal changes after giving birth cause mother dogs to shed a great deal of their hair. This is called postpartum effluvium and usually occurs six to eight weeks after whelping (giving birth). This hair loss is normal but the timing couldn't be worse. About the time the breeder might be showing puppies to prospective new buyers and families, the mother of the litter will probably be shedding a lot of hair to the point where she can look unattractive. To the inexperienced person, this hair loss can be misinterpreted as poor health when in fact, postpartum effluvium is a normal occurrence several weeks after whelping.

Shedding and Photoperiod

Dogs that are housed indoors shed year-round, rather than seasonally. This is because the photoperiod (the number of hours of daylight exposure each day) affects shedding more than environmental temperature does. Photoperiod is an important factor in the lives of most species and affects many biological processes, including shedding, reproduction, sleep cycles, melanin production, and changes in pigmentation.

Shih Tzus are usually exposed to several hours of light year-round, because they live indoors and are exposed to artificial lighting, even in winter when there are less hours of sunlight. Although hair is shed throughout the year, not all of the hair is shed at one time. On a Shih Tzu's body, different hairs are in different stages of growth. Dogs typically shed in a mosaic pattern throughout the body. For this reason, daily brushing is very important for a Shih Tzu. Brushing removes dead hairs, stimulates the skin and distributes natural oils in the coat.

Supplies

Ready to Groom

When you are ready to seriously begin grooming, you should have all of your supplies handy before you begin. These include
• A grooming table
• Nonslip mat and towels
• A soft brush
• A brush with flexible pins
• A fine slicker brush
• A comb with rotating pins
• A comb that is fine on one end and coarse on the other (teeth spacing)
• A parting comb
• A rake comb
• Scissors (blunt-tipped, especially for wiggly puppies)
• Nail trimmers

• A spray bottle
• Bows and elastic bands
• Hair gel, hair spray
• Cornstarch
• Emollient shampoo (pH balanced for dog skin)
• Gentle hair rinse (developed for dogs)
• Self-rinse shampoo
• Ear-cleaning solution (available from your veterinarian)
• Cotton-tipped swabs, cotton balls
• Washcloth
• Paper towels
• Hair dryer
• Electric hair clippers
• Extra clipper blades (#4, #5, #7, #10, #15)
• Electric nail sander (optional)

Grooming Is Fun

Grooming your Shih Tzu should be fun. It should not be a chore. It should always be a positive experience for Lotus and an enjoyable activity for you. It is a way for you and your companion to enjoy each other's company and strengthen the human-animal bond you share, the bond that is so precious to you both and central to your mutual friendship. Grooming is also a time to relax. Many Shih Tzu owners groom their dogs as a form of relaxation and artistic expression. It is a documented fact that people can lower their blood pressure simply by touching or caressing an animal. Lotus will enjoy the massage sensation and skin stimulation a good

Grooming should be fun and enjoyable for you and your Shih Tzu. You may sit or stand, just be sure to always work at a height that is comfortable for you.

brushing provides and benefit from the close human contact and special attention received during grooming sessions.

If you plan to show Lotus in the conformation ring, you will not only have to become an expert handler, but a skilled groomer, unless you choose to hire a professional handler or groomer to do these tasks for you so you can sit at ringside and admire Lotus as he competes.

Shih Tzu owners develop their own individual grooming methods that work best for them and give them the desired results for their particular dogs. You can master the art of grooming Lotus to perfection only

after learning from accomplished Shih Tzu breeders, handlers, and groomers and after countless hours of practice.

If you don't like the idea of grooming, a Shih Tzu is not the dog for you. It is true you have other options, such as taking your pet to a professional groomer, but is that realistic? Do you have the time and finances to hire and commute to a groomer as often as your pet will need one? If you do not have the time, or are not inclined to learn proper grooming techniques, now is the time to consider a different breed, no matter how much you love Shih Tzus. A Shih Tzu requires grooming and lots

No fair! Messy hair! With some practice and artistic skill you can make your puppy look like an aristocrat! It's fun to do!

of it. If you are unable to provide this necessary care for your pet, then don't get a Shih Tzu.

Hair care doesn't require hours every day, but it does require daily attention. If Lotus is tidy and doesn't play in fields or other areas containing weeds, burrs, parasites, and dirt, you can keep him in nice condition with a few minutes of daily brushing. Unless you are willing to do the detail work yourself, you will still have to take Lotus to a professional groomer on a regular basis (a *minimum* of once every three weeks is recommended). You can also have your pet body-clipped. Although the clipped look doesn't have the esthetic appeal or impact of a spectacular, long coat, it is practical and easier to care for and to keep clean. It is also a lot cooler in the summer.

Grooming sessions are the perfect time to thoroughly inspect Lotus's skin to be sure it is healthy and to check for signs of dry or oily skin, lumps and bumps, parasites, stickers, scabs, knots, and mats.

Eye check: During the grooming sessions you should also check the eyes and ears. The eyes should always be clear and bright. It is not unusual for Shih Tzus to suffer from eye irritation due to hairs coming in contact with, or sticking to, the eyes. Take this opportunity to trim away stray hairs that may be a problem. If Lotus's eyes frequently tear, contact your veterinarian immediately. Prolonged tearing is a sign of other eye problems and the cause needs to be diagnosed and treated right away. Many eye problems in the Shih Tzu can lead rapidly to blindness if not treated early. Excessive tearing can also stain the hair around the inner corners of the eyes and turn the hair a dark, reddish brown color. Your

Ready to go out and see the world—and be seen!

veterinarian can provide you with a product developed specifically for use around the eyes that can help eliminate the stain. More important, your veterinarian can determine the cause of tearing and treat it appropriately, before it becomes a serious problem.

Getting Started

If you want your Shih Tzu to always look and feel its very best, daily grooming is essential. All Shih Tzus need to be combed, brushed, and bathed routinely to keep their coats healthy, shiny, and free of mats. Grooming is not just for cosmetic purposes. If the coat becomes matted, its insulating quality will be lost. Mats are good hiding places for parasites, such as fleas, ticks, and mites. Because severely matted hair cannot be untangled, you will have to cut them out with scissors, and this will make your companion look

uneven and ragged. By regularly brushing and bathing Lotus, you can observe his overall appearance and condition on a daily basis by checking the skin, eyes, ears, teeth, and nails. You can detect signs of problems (irritated, tearing eyes; foul-smelling ears; lumps, parasites, and sores) early, before they become a serious health problem.

Training Your Puppy to Be Groomed

Don't wait until your Shih Tzu is an adolescent with a mind of his own before you begin training him to be groomed. Begin training immediately, while Lotus is still a puppy. A puppy may object to brushes and combs in the beginning, but he will quickly learn to accept daily hair care, especially if you give him lots of praise and keep grooming sessions short. Make sure you end the grooming session before Lotus tires of it and starts to misbehave. If he objects and struggles and you stop grooming, you will only reinforce bad behavior. Lotus will think that if he doesn't cooperate, you will give up. Make sure your puppy knows who is boss. Be gentle, kind, consistent, yet firm, and always end on a positive note.

There are several things you can do to make training easier:

• Take your puppy out for a walk or play with him in the backyard. Let him burn up some energy so he is a bit tired before you start. (Don't wear him out, though!) A tired puppy is less likely to put up a fight.

• Then begin by placing Lotus on your lap and caressing his head, face, and ears in a soothing, calming manner. Alternate handling each of his feet. Make it a pleasant experience.

• Gently place a brush on his back. At first your puppy will want to examine the object or maybe chew on it. Once the curiosity has passed, try to gently brush his back. As Lotus accepts this contact, you may gently and lightly brush the top of his head, his legs, and his tail. In between times, rub his belly and scratch his ears.

• Keep the first sessions very short, three to five minutes in length, and end while Lotus is still enjoying the attention. Consider giving a small food reward to signal good behavior and the end of the grooming session.

Table Training

You will find that grooming your Shih Tzu is a lot of fun and a very enjoyable activity for both of you, if your companion is trained to lie down or stand still on a grooming table and cooperate. A grooming table allows you to work in various positions at a comfortable level, without bending or stooping, and to obtain the best aesthetic results.

If Lotus is not accustomed to a grooming table and is not obedient, you will lose control of the grooming session and that can lead to some clumsy—even dangerous—situations. Before you can groom him, he must be trained to sit, lie down, and stand quietly on the table. The key to success is to be gentle and patient, yet firm. Start by placing a rubber nonslip mat on the tabletop. Cover the mat with a towel and stand Lotus on the mat.

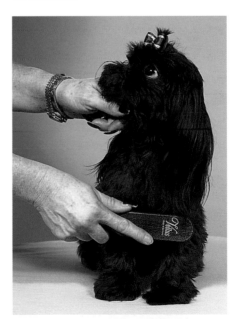

Train your puppy to sit, stand, and lie down on the table. This makes it possible for you to groom all areas of your pet's body.

• If your Shih Tzu is just a puppy, begin by making him lie on his side. He will struggle a bit and try to get up. Some Shih Tzus can be quite stubborn so the wrestling match may last a while! Hold on gently and firmly until he has stopped squirming. If he yelps and cries, speak to him reassuringly, but continue to gently hold him so he remains lying on his side.

Important: *Do not restrain your Shih Tzu by the skin on the back of his neck and do not pull tightly on the skin around his eyes, ears, or neck. Excessive force could cause the eyes to proptose (bulge out of their sockets), requiring immediate emergency veterinary care to put the eyes back in place and to prevent blindness.*

• When Lotus has calmed down, begin by gently brushing him with a soft brush. At this point don't worry about brushing out every knot and tangle. Just work on getting him accustomed to the procedure.

• After your puppy understands he must lie quietly on his side while you brush him, you can teach him to stand on the grooming table (this would be several lessons later). To do this, hold Lotus lightly with your hand between the rear legs. If he tries to move or sit down, apply gentle pressure to bring him back to the right position. Don't try to position Lotus by lifting him under the stomach. This will cause him to hunch up. Speak reassuringly in a happy voice and pet your puppy. Make these first training sessions short, no longer than five minutes.

• When you are finished, give Lotus lots of praise for cooperating and a small food reward, and set him on the floor. This is your way of letting him know that his time on the table has ended. If desired, you can repeat these mini-training sessions two or three times a day until your Shih Tzu feels comfortable and happy standing on the table.

Handling, Brushing, and Combing Your Shih Tzu

Once your pet is accustomed to lying or standing on the grooming table and remains still without trying to jump off the table, you can begin training him to be handled, brushed, and combed. Begin by gently lifting and holding each foot for a few seconds. As Lotus becomes used to having his feet handled, you can hold each foot for longer periods of time

After your puppy has become accustomed to you holding and touching his feet, you can trim excess hairs from between the pads.

and handle each toe individually (as you will have to do later when you trim the toenails). Gently handle the ears, face, body, and tail. When Lotus accepts your handling calmly and remains on the table, you can introduce him to a soft brush or a gentle comb. You will also have to use the spray bottle and lightly spray the coat. At first, the spray bottle may startle your puppy. You may need to spend a little extra time reassuring him so he becomes accustomed to the sound and sensation of the sprayer.

At this point, you may not succeed in completely combing or brushing out all the dirt or tangles, but your puppy is getting used to objects touching his body. Place the brush lightly on his back and sides and then begin to gently brush the surface of the coat. Don't worry about the face and ears right now. If Lotus seems to enjoy the massage, continue for a few more minutes. Be sure to stop before he tires of it. If you are training a very young animal, remember that they bore easily so you may want to limit this session to three to five minutes.

Working Around the Face and Toenails

You may begin working on and around your pet's face once he has learned to accept having his body brushed and combed. Make sure Lotus is well trained before you work with scissors or other objects near his eyes and ears. Blunt-tipped scissors are recommended.

The finished product! Nice and tidy feet do not track mud and dirt as easily. After every walk, always check the feet for mats, stickers, grass awns, pebbles, and other foreign objects that can cause discomfort.

• Start by scratching the ears and under the chin. Take a soft cotton cloth or tissue and gently wipe the corners of the eyes, the muzzle, and then the corners of the nostrils.
• Lift the lips and open the mouth. Try to perform these activities in the same order. Make them a brief, but repetitive, routine followed by plenty of praise.
• Continue to handle and lift the feet. If all is proceeding well, now is a good time to pretend to use the nail clippers. Let your pup become familiar with the sound the clippers make, set them on the nails, but do not cut the nails.

It will take several sessions before Lotus has completely adapted to the routine of lying or standing on the grooming table and being handled, brushed, and combed.

Your Shih Tzu should be well-trained before you attempt to groom areas around the face, especially when using sharp or pointed objects.

Clipping

When you think Lotus is ready, you can introduce him to the electric clippers. Don't try to clip the coat. Simply turn on the clippers so that he can get used to the sound. You can remove the clipper blades and practice setting the clippers against your puppy's body so that he can become familiar with the sensation.

Bathing Your Shih Tzu

On average, you should bathe Lotus at least once every three weeks. Some Shih Tzus require a bath once a week. Use a pH balanced shampoo developed for canines that is gentle on the skin. *Don't use hair products designed for humans.*

For frequent bathing, an emollient shampoo is recommended. An emollient doesn't contain soaps, rinses out easily, and is very gentle on a Shih Tzu's delicate skin. Emollient shampoos can be purchased from your veterinarian or pet supply store.

Shih Tzus fit easily inside most sinks or bathtubs. If you use a sink, make sure the faucets are out of the way, so Lotus doesn't bump into them and get injured (a common accident). Also, be sure the water is set at a comfortable temperature *before* you put Lotus in the sink or use the sprayer to rinse him.

Drying

Eventually, you can train Lotus so you can use a hair dryer on his coat. Although many owners prefer to towel-dry their Shih Tzus after bathing, a hair dryer can speed up the job and produce beautiful results. While drying the coat you can also inspect the skin, as the dryer separates the hairs. Begin by simply turning on the dryer on a low setting and holding it away from your pet. If Lotus is startled and wants to run away, pet him and talk to him soothingly until he calms down. Do not use the dryer on the coat yet. At each grooming session to follow, turn on the dryer and hold it away from your dog. When Lotus is no longer bothered by the sound of the dryer (this may take several sessions), you can begin by lightly spraying water on the coat and setting the dryer to low to gently blow air on the back. Eventually, your Shih Tzu will get used to the hair dryer and you may use it on the sides, shoulders, and neck. Always make sure the setting is low and the temperature is not hot.

Lengthening Grooming Sessions

When you are both ready (and not before!), you can lengthen grooming sessions and begin to seriously groom the coat. Be careful when you work around the eyes.

Note: *To avoid accident or injury, use only blunt-tipped scissors and cover the eyes with your hand when you trim stray hairs away from the face and eyes.*

Pay attention to the feet, trim away excess hair, and keep the toenails at a reasonable length. The grooming table is also a good place to brush your pet's teeth. You can learn many tricks of the trade from other Shih Tzu owners or professional dog groomers. The more you practice, the more skilled you will become, and the better your little "lion dog" will look!

Tubs: If you have more than one Shih Tzu, or are becoming a serious groomer, consider buying a tub made especially for dog grooming. Many of these specially designed dog tubs have the advantage of being at a comfortable working height and provide easy methods of restraint, stairs to climb in and out of the tub, heavy-duty sprayers to rinse the coat, and an area to place your grooming products.

• Place a hair trap over the drain to catch loose hairs and put a nonslip mat in the bottom of the sink.

• Adjust the water to a comfortable temperature and wet the coat.

• If your Shih Tzu has a flea problem, begin by wetting the head and working down the body to the tip of the tail. When a dog is submerged in water, or the coat gets wet, fleas have a tendency to climb toward higher ground, in this case, the head. If you don't start by washing the head, you will find the fleas congregated around the eyes, ears, and muzzle shortly after you begin. By washing the head first, you can suds and rinse the fleas down the body and into the bathwater. On the other hand, if Lotus doesn't have a flea problem, you might prefer to start the bath from the bottom up, ending with the head. When Shih Tzus get their heads wet, or when water goes in their ears, they shake themselves vigorously to dry off. You don't want your pet shaking and spraying you with water while you are trying to wash him. Begin by putting some clean cotton in Lotus's ears to help keep water from getting into the ear canals. This will minimize head shaking and ear infections.

• Mix some emollient shampoo with warm water so that the mixture is a comfortable temperature before you apply it to the coat.

• Wash the coat well and rinse it thoroughly with warm (not hot) water. Give Lotus a second wash and after the final rinse, pour a mixture of crème rinse and warm water over the coat and work it in well. Rinse again, leaving in just enough of the rinse that the coat feels barely slick (not sticky or gooey), and gently squeeze as much water as possible out of the coat.

• After you bathe Lotus, make sure he does not become chilled. Blot excess water from his coat with a towel. Then wrap him in another thick, large towel and dry him thoroughly. Dry the ears well with a soft, dry cloth. You can use a cotton-tipped swab to dry and clean the ear canals, but be sure you do not go too deeply or you could rupture the eardrum (tympanic membrane). Make sure Lotus's ears are dried out as well as possible after his bath. Germs grow rapidly in moist ears and Shih Tzus are prone to bacterial and fungal infections of the ears.

• To dry Lotus's coat, begin by blotting excess water with a towel and then blow-drying with a hair dryer. Separate the hair in strands or layers as you dry it. There are several excellent hair dryers designed for dog grooming. Using a hair dryer will make the coat appear to be fuller and have more body.

Grooming Styles

There are many ways you can groom your Shih Tzu. The "casual look" is ideal for the Shih Tzu that stays at home and goes on family outings. The "show look" requires a lot more time and grooming skill, and is what is expected of the Shih Tzu on exhibit competing in the conformation ring. A short haircut or body clip is great for the practical-minded owner who has time for only a low-maintenance coat.

Even if Lotus isn't competing in the show ring, he will always be Best in Show at your house! So here's how to groom him accordingly.

1. Spray Lotus lightly with water and a small amount of gentle hair rinse or crème conditioner designed for canines and recommended by your veterinarian, breeder, or experienced Shih Tzu owners. Always spray lightly before you begin. Brushing or combing dry hair will cause the hair to break.

After every bath, make sure to dry your Shih Tzu thoroughly and keep him warm.

2. Gently and thoroughly brush through the coat. Be sure to separate the hair down to the skin so that all tangles and knots are removed. If you brush Lotus daily, large mat formation can be avoided. Mats are difficult to comb out and large mats almost always must be removed with scissors.

3. Pay particular attention to the axillary region (under the front limbs), groin area (inside of thighs), belly, behind and under the ears, and below the anus. These areas tend to become matted or soiled and are often overlooked.

4. Always brush Lotus thoroughly *before* you give him a bath. If you don't remove knots, tangles, and mats before you bathe your pet, they will become fixed in the coat when it gets wet and will be even more difficult to remove later.

5. Express the anal sacs *before* you bathe Lotus. Anal sacs are located at either side of the inside of the rectum. They feel like small grapes and contain a foul-smelling substance. If the sacs are not expressed, or emptied, on a regular basis, they can become impacted, infected, or abscessed, and rupture. Always express the anal sacs just *before* a bath, so Lotus doesn't smell offensive!

How to express anal sacs:
• Wear disposable gloves.
• Place an absorbent tissue over the anus (to avoid being sprayed).
• Feel for the sac through the perianal tissue on each side of the anus (they feel like small grapes).

Brush your Shih Tzu thoroughly before you give it a bath.

• Gently squeeze on the sacs from the outside of the anus, with your thumb and index finger, until they empty into the tissue. Anal sac contents are normally brown in color and may range in consistency from liquid to pasty.

Your veterinarian or groomer can show you the proper way to express the anal sacs.

6. Clean Lotus's face carefully and gently. If you are using a self-rinse shampoo to cleanse the area around the muzzle and mustache, be very careful that it doesn't get in his eyes.

7. Gently wipe debris away from the inner corner of Lotus's eyes, using

Wipe debris and hair away from the corners of the eyes. Eyes should be bright and clear. Tearing can be a sign of eye problems.

a clean, damp washcloth. Wipe from the inner corner of the eye downward and outward. If your pet's eyes frequently tear, contact your veterinarian. Prolonged tearing can be a sign of serious eye problems; it can also stain the hair around the inner corners of the eyes a dark, reddish brown color. Your veterinarian can provide you with a product developed specifically for use around the eyes that can help eliminate the stain, but more important, your veterinarian can determine the cause of tearing and treat it appropriately, before it becomes a serious problem.

8. Comb the hair gently away from Lotus's eyes *every day*. Loose hairs come in contact with the eyes and stick to the surface of the eye. Continual irritation from hairs can cause serious, painful conditions, such as dry eyes, infections, corneal ulcers, and blindness. Let your pet's hair grow between the eyes and at the base of the muzzle (the bridge of the nose) until it is long enough to tie up in a topknot. Do not trim these hairs unless absolutely necessary because they will require constant trimming to keep short or they will stick into the eyes and injure them. While you are letting the hair on Lotus's face grow long, keep it combed away from the eyes until it is long enough to tie up in a topknot.

9. If your Shih Tzu has hair and debris in his eyes, rinse them daily with a gentle eyewash recommended by your veterinarian. Do not use an eye product prescribed for yourself or for your other pets. Do not use products in the eyes that contain corticosteroids unless your veterinarian has specifically prescribed them for Lotus to treat his current eye condition. If you are purchasing an eye rinse over the counter at your local pharmacy, make sure you do not accidentally purchase a contact lens *cleaning* solution.

Note: *If your Shih Tzu is squinting, has reddened scleras (the normally white parts of the eyes), pale blue areas on the surface of either or both eyes, is tearing, or has a discharge from the eyes, contact your veterinarian immediately.*

10. Clean around the muzzle, particularly at the bridge of the nose and where it comes in contact with the face between the eyes. Some Shih Tzus have a tendency to develop moist areas at the base of the muzzle and these areas can have a foul odor.

11. You can trim excess hair from the ear canals by pulling or plucking them. When you clean the inside of your dog's ears, use a soft cloth. Do not use gauze because this could be harsh on delicate tissues. If you use cotton-swabbed tips, do not stick them deep into the ear canal. Avoid ear-cleaning products containing alcohol unless your veterinarian has recommended them. Alcohol is very drying and can be painful on raw, tender, or inflamed areas. If you see

any discharge from the ear or smell any foul odors from the ear, contact your veterinarian immediately. Ear problems are very painful and may lead to hearing loss and problems balancing.

12. Trim excess hair from between the footpads with blunt-tipped scissors and trim around the feet level with the grooming table to give them a rounded appearance. Neat, trimmed feet look very tidy and prevent mats, dirt, foreign objects (such as grass awns or "foxtails"), and excess moisture (leading to bacterial growth, moist dermatitis, and sores) from accumulating between the toes. Lotus will walk more comfortably and track less dirt and debris into your home.

13. Trim excess hair away from the groin area and under the tail with blunt-tipped scissors or a #10 or #15 clipper blade.

14. Trim the toenails (see page 88) and if Lotus's dewclaws (vestigial

Trim the hair to emphasize a rounded head.

digits located where a "thumb" would be) have not been surgically removed, remember to trim those as well. If left untrimmed, dewclaws can snag and tear or grow so long that they spiral around and imbed into surrounding tissue. Both conditions are painful.

Topknots and Trims

The type of topknot and trim you select for Lotus will depend on how long his hair is, and how much time you have to spend on grooming, convenience, and practicality. It also matters what your pet will be doing. For example, will he be lounging in the living room or will he be on the show circuit?

Decide as soon as possible if Lotus is going to be a show dog. That "show-stopper" coat necessary to win in the show ring cannot be grown overnight and you'll need a head start on it. From the very beginning it must be groomed, maintained, and protected. Shih Tzus destined for the show ring do not run loose in the yard, take walks in the park, or play rough and tumble with other dogs. They do not spend time on carpeting (carpeting is abrasive to the coat and the static electricity buildup can break the fine hairs). The show Shih Tzu is raised in such a manner that the coat is protected at all times. Anything that could damage the coat is strictly avoided. Shih Tzus are housed in clean exercise pens and long hair may be wrapped to prevent it from dragging, breaking, or becoming soiled. Long hairs on the face are wrapped and many Shih Tzus are provided water in a water bottle to

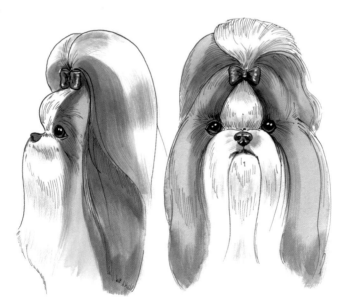

A topknot adds grace and elegance to a Shih Tzu's appearance and helps keep hairs from falling into the eyes.

help keep the hair on the face clean and dry. There's no doubt about it: If you intend to exhibit your Shih Tzu, plan on a great deal of work and grooming to maintain the coat in luxurious condition. When Lotus has completed his show career, you will probably welcome a new low-maintenance hairstyle for him, such as one of the short body clips.

There are several types of topknots, body trims, leg trims, and tail trims for Shih Tzus. Certain styles of leg trims go best with particular types of body trims. With practice and experience, you will discover which topknots, trims, and cuts show off your pet's qualities and hide his minor flaws, producing the balanced, beautiful look of the classic Shih Tzu.

Topknots:

• *Puppies.* Puppies look cutest if their hair is cut to emphasize their rounded heads. The topknot is cut with scissors so that all the hairs are about 2 inches (4 cm) long. The beard and mustache are left to grow longer, up to 6 inches (12 cm), and the ears are trimmed to blend in with the facial hair so that the head appears round.

• *Kennel cut.* Shave all of the hair except for over the forehead. Cut the forehead hair and trim the ears with scissors to create a rounded skull appearance. Be sure to blend the ears in well with the sides of the head. Keep the hair out of the eyes but do not trim the base of the muz-

The puppy cut is simple, cute, and easy to maintain.

zle. Another variation of this cut is to allow the hair to grow all over the top of the head and keep it trimmed with scissors to a length of 1 to 2 inches (2.5 to 5 cm) to form a full topknot. Comb and trim the ears and beard to emphasize a rounded appearance.

Most puppies won't have hair long enough for a topknot until they are five or six months of age. The topknot styles you create for your Shih Tzu are limited only by your imagination. You can trim the topknot to various lengths or you can let it grow long. You can part the topknot and secure it to the ears with elastics, plastics, or bows. It's fun to select bows that go well with your pet's coat color.

To make the topknot stand up higher, you can comb it straight back, tease it gently, section it, band it, and curl it with a curling iron (as is done for the show ring). Curling and teasing, plus a dab of hair gel, give the topknot more support to help it stand up higher on the head so that the neck looks longer and graceful.

Trim your puppy's head in a way that accentuates the flat face and rounded head.

6 inches (7.5 to 15 cm) long. The puppy trim lets your puppy keep a full tail along with a cut that emphasizes a pretty body and cylindrical legs, all in a hair length ranging from 1 to 3 inches (2.5 to 5 cm). Your puppy may have shorter hair and a lower-maintenance trim but he still requires daily brushing.

Kennel clip: This is the easiest haircut to maintain because most of the hair has been removed. All of the body is clipped (with a #4, #5, or #7 clipper blade), except for the end of the tail, which ends in a tuft, and a tuft of hair over the skull to emphasize the head's rounded appearance. The feet and ears are trimmed and that's all there is to it. This is a great haircut for the summertime and an ideal haircut for owners who have little time or desire to groom their Shih Tzus.

Body clip: The body is clipped with a #4, #5, #7, #10, or #15 blade. The hair on the back is trimmed short and the legs are trimmed to a 1- to 2-inch (2.5 to 5 cm) length and shaped and belled to flare out at the feet. The tail is trimmed at the base and left intact for the length of its curvature. The head is trimmed to accentuate a rounded look, the beard is maintained, and the ears are trimmed to a bell shape to complement the leg

• *Puppy trim.* For the Shih Tzu puppy that has a thick coat and enjoys playing outdoors and getting dirty but still should look cute, this might be the style to choose. It is cool in summer and warm enough in winter. The hair on the head is trimmed 1 to 2 inches (2.5 to 5 cm) all over and the ears are trimmed to blend in with the head. As always, the goal in shaping the head is to emphasize its rounded appearance. The beard is left 3 to

The kennel clip is the easiest haircut to maintain because most of the hair has been removed.

The body clip is a chic summer style that is embellished by bell-shaped legs and ears and a showy tail.

It may be called the Schnauzer cut, but the beard, short topknot, and tassel tail add charm that is unmistakably Shih Tzu.

trim. This is another great summer style with easy upkeep.

Schnauzer cut: With this cut, the Shih Tzu is trimmed with a #5, #7, #10, or #15 blade, from the skull down the neck and to the chest and body, with the trim going in the direction of hair growth. The clipper trim stops at the bottom of the rib cage and the bottom one third of the legs. The hairs from these areas are trimmed with scissors to a cylindrical shape and left 1 to 2 inches (2.5 to 5 cm) long. The beard is maintained, and the ears are lightly trimmed to offset a short topknot. The tail is left in a tassel.

Cocker cut: The Cocker cut lets your Shih Tzu keep more of its hair than most cuts and gives a sense of overall balance. The body is clipped with a #5, #7, #10, or #15 blade, from the top of the back of the neck to the base of the tail. If you imagine a parting down the center of your Shih Tzu's

back and perpendicular to the parting about one third of the way down the side of the body (to the top of the forelimb), that's where the clipping ends. From that point on, the chest hairs and hairs on the sides of the body and the leg hairs are trimmed about 4 to

The Cocker cut retains more hair than most styles and gives your pet a balanced and bold, yet classy, appearance.

5 inches (10 to 15 cm) in length. The legs are tapered down to the feet, the ears are rounded, and the tail is flagged.

Full furnishings clip: Furnishings refer to all the long hair responsible for embellishing and accentuating the look for which the breed is recognized. Furnishings include the beard and topknot and long hairs on the ears, limbs (also called skirts or pants on the hindquarters), belly, face, and tail.

In the full furnishings clip, only the neck and back are clipped (in a Cocker-style clip) and the legs, sides of the body, and tail are left full length or trimmed level with the grooming table.

This style is difficult to maintain and requires the most time and work. When properly maintained, it is also the most esthetically appealing and impressive style.

The full furnishings clip is for the ambitious individual, willing and able to maintain a long, flowing coat. Only the neck and back are clipped, the rest of the coat is left full length.

Show Ring Ready

If you are going to exhibit your Shih Tzu, you will be very busy grooming him on a regular basis, with special attention to details on show days. The show Shih Tzu is shown in *full coat*.

1. Brush the coat thoroughly and part it down the center of the back, along the spine, with a parting comb or a knitting needle.

2. Trim the hair on the legs in layers, level with the grooming table and remove the hair from between the footpads.

3. Trim around the feet and under the tail.

Ironing

Many Shih Tzu exhibitors use a padded iron designed for use in dogs to remove unwanted waviness and straighten the coat. If you use an iron on your pet's coat, be sure to dampen the hair before each use and work quickly so you do not to burn and damage the hair. Comb out your pet's hair in sections and iron each section individually. Ironing several small sections of hair produces better results than ironing large clumps of hair.

• Divide the topknot into two sections, front and back. Do not pull up hair from the ears to include in the topknot.

• Gently tease the backside of the sections and then gently smooth over the hairs on top. Fasten the sections with elastic bands and fasten the two sections together.

Ready for the show ring or ready to show off—lots of grooming keeps your Shih Tzu looking wonderful!

• With a curling iron, curl the ends of the sections so that they do not fall forward, into your pet's eyes.

• Place a bow at the base of the front section to hide the elastic bands. Some exhibitors use hairspray to keep the topknot in place. If you decide to use hairspray, be sure to cover your pet's eyes to protect them when you spray. You might prefer to use a small amount of light hair gel instead to keep the topknot in place. Hair can easily come undone as you run around the ring, proudly showing off your Shih Tzu.

Tips

In summary, here are a few tips to make the grooming session a safe and enjoyable experience for you and your Shih Tzu:

1. *Remember that several short training sessions are better than one long one.* Limit puppy grooming to three to five minutes. Puppies have short attention spans and bore or tire easily.

2. Begin training for grooming as soon as possible. The day after you bring your puppy home is not too soon.

3. Designate an area to use exclusively for grooming. This should be an easy-to-clean, convenient location, close to an electrical outlet (for hair dryer, clippers, electric nail files, and vacuum cleaner).

4. Select a location with good lighting, so you can see what you're doing.

5. Select a table that is high enough for you to work at a comfortable height, depending on whether you prefer to work sitting or standing.

6. Make sure the table surface is nonslip, to prevent falls or injury.

7. When your Shih Tzu requires a reprimand, use the word "*No*" consistently.

8. Never use your pet's name in connection with a reprimand.

9. Train by using positive reinforcements (praise or food rewards) and not by negative reinforcement (scolding, physical punishment).

10. Invest in the best. Purchase quality tools and equipment, particularly brushes, combs, scissors (blunt-tipped and thinning), and nail clippers. This will reduce your chances of developing blisters on your fingers, or sore wrists and arms from overexertion.

11. Place all the grooming items near the grooming table, within easy reach.

12. Use only products designed for dogs to ensure a pH balance for canine skin, including emollient shampoos, spray-on dry shampoos, or self-rinse shampoos. Do not use products containing parasiticides (flea and tick killers) unless specifically prescribed by your veterinarian. These products are harsh on the skin and can be harmful for small dogs, especially young puppies.

13. Always praise your Shih Tzu for good performance and behavior. Give a small food reward at the conclusion of each grooming session and take your pet for a walk afterward, whenever possible. Your dog will associate grooming with other pleasant experiences and look forward to the next grooming session.

14. *Never leave any animal unattended on the table.*

The time and effort you invest in Lotus's coat and skin will keep him looking in top condition. As you become more familiar with the Shih Tzu standard and develop more skill at grooming, you will find ways to groom your dog so that you can enhance his features to more closely reflect the ideal Shih Tzu.

Toenail Care

Unlike hair that grows in phases, toenails grow continuously. Shih Tzus need to have their toenails clipped regularly, especially because they spend most of their time indoors and don't wear down their nails on hard surfaces. Check the nails frequently and don't let them become overgrown. They will probably need to be trimmed at least once a month. You can ask your veterinarian or groomer to trim Lotus's toenails, or you can do it yourself.

Toenail trimming is something most dog owners dread, but it really isn't difficult. If you work with your dog's feet from the time he is very young, he will not mind having his feet handled and restrained. It is important to keep the nails trimmed so that they do not snag or tear, causing him pain or discomfort. If the nails become too overgrown, they will eventually deform the paws, interfere with movement, and hinder

Lotus's ability to walk. In the most severe cases, overgrown toenails can curve under and pierce the foot-pads.

To determine if Lotus needs a nail trim, stand him on the grooming table. None of the nails should touch the surface of the table. You will notice each toenail curves and tapers into a point. If the toenail is not too dark in color, you will be able to see pink inside of the toenail, or the "quick." This is the blood supply and just below it is the excess nail growth that you will remove. If the toenails are too dark to differentiate where the quick ends, you can illuminate the nail with a penlight or a flashlight to find the line of demarcation where the blood supply ends.

Nail Trimming

There are different types of nail trimmers. Most Shih Tzu owners prefer the guillotine-style clippers. To use these you place the toenail inside the metal loop, aligning the upper and lower blades with the area you wish to cut, and squeeze the clipper handles. A good rule of thumb is to cut only the very tip of the toenail. If the nail is still too long, continue to remove the end of the nail carefully in small increments. If you accidentally cut too close, you can stop the bleeding by applying styptic powder (a clotting powder commercially available from your pet store or veterinarian) or styptic sticks (human shaving sticks). If you don't have styptic powder, cornstarch may be helpful or you may be able to stop

Nail care is very important. Cut the tip of the nail where it starts to curve.

the bleeding by pushing the end of the toenail into a piece of wax or a dry bar of a mild soap. This will serve as a plug until the bleeding stops. You can also stop the bleeding by applying pressure to the nail with a clean cloth for five minutes.

When the blades of the nail trimmers become dull they should be replaced so they do not break, shred, or crack the nails. You can also buy an electric toenail filer to round off and smooth the nails after trimming. Be sure to always praise Lotus for his cooperation. Without it, nail trimming is virtually impossible!

Dental Care

Regular dental care and tooth brushing are very important aspects of your Shih Tzu's health care program and should start in early puppyhood.

Puppies, like babies, are born without teeth. When Shih Tzus reach three to four weeks of age, their deciduous teeth (baby teeth) start to erupt. At around four months, these twenty-eight temporary teeth begin to fall out and are replaced with forty-eight permanent teeth. During this time, puppies want to chew on everything, just like a human baby who is teething, and it is important to provide your puppy with lots of safe chew toys. By the time Lotus is six months old, all of the adult teeth should be in place. These teeth must last a lifetime, so it is important to take good care of them by preventing plaque and tartar buildup and periodontal disease.

Plaque: Plaque is a coating on the teeth caused by a combination of bacteria, saliva, and decaying food. As plaque builds up, a cementlike substance called tartar develops, usually starting at the gum line. It is yellow to brown in color and can eventually spread to cover the entire tooth. Periodontal disease develops as bacteria infect the root of the tooth and cause erosion of the surrounding bone that secures the tooth. Eventually, the root is destroyed and the tooth will fall out, or require extraction. Periodontal disease causes more problems than bad breath, swollen, painful, bleeding gums, and tooth loss. The bacteria present in the mouth and gums can enter the bloodstream and grow on the heart valves, causing heart problems, or infect the kidneys and other organs of the body.

Brushing: The best way to reduce plaque buildup is by dental brushing. It is easy for your pet to become used to the idea of regular brushing if you start when he is a puppy. Baby teeth are good for practice and training. By the time his adult teeth are in, Lotus will be used to the daily routine.

Purchase a soft-bristle toothbrush and dog toothpaste recommended by your veterinarian or local pet supply store. *Do not use human toothpaste.* Many human products contain spearmint or peppermint or other substances that cause dogs to salivate (drool) profusely or that will upset their stomachs. Use warm water. Cold water is unpleasant and

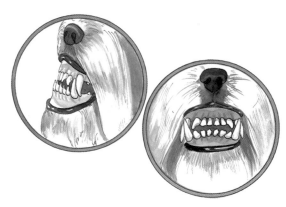

Check your pet's mouth regularly to make sure that the teeth are free of tartar and that the gums are healthy. Be sure to open the mouth wide enough to examine the molars in the back of the jaw.

may temporarily turn the gums and tongue bluish in color.

• Start with the upper front teeth (incisors), brushing down and away from the gum line, and proceed back to the premolars and molars on one side of the mouth. You may also brush these teeth in a gentle, circular motion. Repeat on the upper teeth on the opposite side of the mouth.

• When you brush the bottom teeth, pay particular attention to the incisors. Shih Tzus are undershot to a certain degree. This means that the lower jaw (mandible) protrudes or extends in front of the upper jaw (maxilla). They also may have a missing tooth or slightly misaligned teeth. Keep this in mind when you look for possible problem areas as you brush.

• From the incisors, work back to the molars, brushing up and away from the gum line. Repeat on the lower teeth on the opposite side of the mouth. Be patient. You may want to break the daily brushing into two sessions at the beginning. Spend about one minute on the upper teeth and then praise your pet for good behavior. Later in the day you can spend another one-minute time increment on the bottom teeth, followed by profuse praise.

Good home dental care is a necessity, but it is not a replacement for veterinary dental visits. Even with the best of care, most dogs require

Brush your pet's teeth regularly. If you start when your Shih Tzu is a puppy, it will quickly learn to accept this important part of its health care.

routine professional dental cleaning and polishing.

Remember: bad breath is *not* normal for a dog. If Lotus has bad breath, he may have periodontal disease or an infection of the mouth, throat, or nasal passages.

Possible Causes of Halitosis
• Periodontal disease
• Foreign body obstructing nasal passages
• Infection or ulcers (tonsils, lips, gums, cheeks, tongue)

Chapter Seven
Feeding Your Shih Tzu

Good nutrition has been recognized for centuries as being one of the most important factors in maintaining health and extending longevity. Of all the countless things you do for your Shih Tzu, providing a nutritionally complete and balanced diet is one of the most important ways to keep your dog healthy throughout life.

When dogs were first domesticated, their meals consisted of remains from the hunt, vegetables from the garden, and whatever "table scraps" were available. Dogs essentially ate much of the same foods as their owners. Due to the wide variety of foods in their meals, most of the nutritional bases were covered. Commercial dog food was not to make its appearance until thousands of years later. Dry kibble became popular during World War II, when meat became a scarce commodity. Later, with consumer convenience in mind as people became more pressed for time, and particularly in the last 40 years, we witnessed the evolution of TV dinners, microwave meals, and fast food restaurants. The dog food business

was not far behind, ready to capitalize on modern-day lifestyles. It was obvious that families that spent less time cooking for themselves were unlikely to cook for the family dog. Through advertising and excellent marketing strategies, the convenience of canned or packaged commercial dog food was promoted until it became commonplace. Today, the manufacture and sale of pet food is a multibillion dollar industry. As with all businesses, profit is a measure of success. This brings us to a key point to keep in mind as we review nutritional choices. Quality nutrition should not cost a fortune, but it certainly is not cheap.

The important role proper nutrition plays in a dog's life cannot be overemphasized. It is the key to overall good health. Fortunately, it is one aspect of Lotus's health care over which you have full control. Don't cut corners when it comes to Lotus's nutrition. Good nutrition will determine his health, development, and life span. With this is mind, let's discuss the kind of nutrition Lotus requires.

Starting Off Right

Before you bring Lotus home, ask the breeder what type of dog food he is currently eating and be sure to obtain at least a two-week supply of the food. Continue feeding the same diet, at least until he has had a chance to adjust to the new family and home. A change in diet during this time of adaptation can be stressful and possibly cause stomach upset or diarrhea. Be sure to take Lotus to your veterinarian within 48 hours of purchase for a physical examination and to plan a complete health care program. The first veterinary visit is an ideal time to discuss specific nutritional requirements and the breeder's recommendations. If a change in diet is appropriate, make the change gradually by increasing the amount of the new diet, and decreasing the amount of the old diet, in small increments at each meal.

Changes in Nutritional Needs

Nutritional needs change throughout life, so it makes sense that Lotus's diet also will need to be changed at times. For example, when he is a puppy, he will need a dog food that provides complete and balanced nutrition for growth and development. As he reaches adolescence, his dietary requirements may lessen or increase, according to his individual needs and activities. When Lotus is an adult, he will have greater nutritional requirements if he is active, doing obedience or agility work, on the show circuit, or being used for breeding purposes, than he would have if he were sedentary. Finally, as Lotus ages, or if he becomes sick or is recovering from an illness, he will need a diet based on his health condition and special needs.

Environment also plays an important role in dietary requirements. Lotus is a housedog. He lives indoors and he lives a life of luxury. He does not have the high caloric requirement of dogs that live in cold weather or work in the fields.

Finally, genetics can influence a dog's caloric requirements, ability to digest and metabolize certain foods, and ability to maintain a normal weight. If some of Lotus's family members have difficulty maintaining an appropriate weight (if they are overweight or underweight), this may be an inherited tendency and you will have to make a special effort to closely monitor his food source and intake.

For each of Lotus's life stages, you should consult your veterinarian to learn which type of dog food would be most beneficial. The ideal nutrition for him today may not be suitable later in life. With increasing consumer awareness, dog food manufacturers continue to make greater efforts to maintain a competitive edge and offer the dog owner a larger, improved selection of dog foods from which to choose. For these reasons, nutrition will always be an important topic of discussion each time you visit your veterinarian.

Dog Food Labels Demystified

Today there are countless brands and types of commercial dog foods on the market. Many claim to be the best food you could possibly offer your pet—but how can you be sure? Dog food comes in all sizes, colors, shapes, and consistencies (dry kibble, semimoist, moist canned). You cannot help but notice how many brands are packaged and named to look and sound more like food for humans than for dogs. This is because the marketing is aimed at you, the consumer. But you are

Feeding your pet a quality, balanced diet is one of the most important things you can do to ensure his health and longevity.

shopping for your dog and he doesn't care what color his food is, he *does* care how it tastes and smells. Even if you buy a very nutritious dog food, it will not benefit Lotus if he refuses to eat it. On the other hand, you don't want to feed an inferior formulation that is not nutritionally balanced simply because he likes the flavor. Sometimes the taste and smell that appeal to a dog are due to food additives, such as artificial flavorings, rather than nutrients.

A good way to select the best dog food for Lotus is to consult with your veterinarian and Shih Tzu breeders. Another way is to study the dog food labels and select a premium dog food that provides complete and balanced nutrition from high-quality protein sources. But be careful! Dog food labels can be confusing and don't always provide exactly the type of information you want. Here are some definitions to help you decipher and interpret dog food labels.

Ingredients

Ingredients include everything that is mixed together to make a specific dog food. Ingredients can be nutritional or have no nutritional value at all. Fat, proteins, carbohydrates, vitamins, and minerals are considered nutritional components of dog food. Nonnutritional ingredients include food additives, artificial coloring, artificial flavorings, and food preservatives.

Dog food labels list ingredients in decreasing order of preponderance by weight. In other words, if the label lists beef, rice, and chicken as ingredients in a given dog food, this means there is more beef than rice or chicken in the mixture, and more rice than chicken in the mixture. However, it does not mean that there is more beef than rice and chicken combined. It also doesn't tell you how much more beef there is than chicken or rice. If beef is listed as the first ingredient, it is possible that there is only slightly more beef in the mixture than rice. It is no wonder dog food labels can be confusing.

The list of ingredients also tells you nothing about the ingredients' quality or digestibility. Different dog food manufacturers may use the same types of ingredients, but the ingredients may vary in quality level. For example, if two different dog foods list chicken as the main ingredient, this doesn't mean the quality of chicken is the same in both brands. It is important to know which brand contains the most nutritious and easily digested parts of chicken. Unfortunately, that information is not always obvious or available and most dog food brands claim to produce the highest-quality dog food. For this reason, you cannot rely solely on the comparison of ingredient labels to select dog food.

Nutrients

Nutrients are substances necessary for life's processes. Some nutrients produce energy, such as sugars, amino acids (the building blocks of proteins), and fatty acids. Other nutrients may not produce energy, but they are required for life just the same. Among the more obvious life-supporting nonenergy-producing nutrients are water, oxygen, vitamins, and minerals. The type and amount of nutrients contained in a dog food mixture make up the nutrient profile.

Nutritional Adequacy

We already know that some dog foods are better than others and that good nutrition is not cheap. So it is not surprising to learn that not all dog foods provide adequate nutrition for all dogs. The American Association of Feed Control Officials (AAFCO) requires dog food companies to demonstrate the nutritional adequacy of their products, either by feeding trials, or by meeting the AAFCO Nutrient Profile. Feeding trials are the preferred method, but most companies simply calculate a formulation for a diet using a standard table of ingredients. Dog food companies are required to make a statement about the nutritional adequacy of all their products (except treats and snacks), such as "complete and balanced nutrition."

Proteins

Certainly the most important health factor in a dog's diet is protein quality. Protein may come from plant or animal sources, but not all proteins are created equally. As a general rule, high-quality animal source proteins are better for dogs than plant source proteins because they provide a better balance of amino

Excellent nutrition is essential to your pet's health. Your puppy will not have a good start in life unless its mother receives a quality diet long before she is bred and during pregnancy, lactation, and weaning.

acids. It is easy to confuse a high percentage of protein in the diet with high-protein quality, but there is a big difference in the definition. You may buy a dog food with a lot of protein, but if the high percentage of protein is of poor quality, your pet will not be able to digest or use much of it.

Animal protein sources found in commercial dog foods include beef, chicken, turkey, duck, lamb, fish, and eggs. However, just because the protein comes from an animal source does not necessarily indicate it is of high nutritional value. You must read the ingredients label closely and look for words such as "meat," "meal," and "by-products." Meat means muscle and skin, with or without bone. By-products include heads, feet, guts, and bone. By-products

are usually less expensive and of poorer-quality protein. Meal tells you the protein source is ground up into particles (as in "cornmeal").

Fats

Fats are important components of your pet's daily diet. They add to the flavor of the food and influence your companion's skin and coat condition. Fats provide energy and play a major role in digestion and the assimilation of fat-soluble vitamins A, D, E, and K. The various fats (animal fat, vegetable oils, olive oil, fish oils) each have different effects on the body and many are used for therapeutic remedies.

Carbohydrates

Carbohydrates are sugars, starches, and fibers. They are an inexpensive source of energy compared to high-quality protein. *Researchers have not yet determined the exact amount of carbohydrates required in the canine diet, yet carbohydrates make up the major portion of today's commercial dog foods.* These carbohydrates usually are provided in the form of corn, cornmeal, rice, or a combination of grains.

Note: Many dogs become allergic to corn, cornmeal, or corn oil in their diets. These allergies often cause serious skin problems.

Because dogs cannot digest fiber, it is used in many dog foods to maintain dry matter bulk. Fiber is used extensively in canine weight-reduction diets. Dogs on a high-fiber diet produce a lot more stool volume than dogs on a high-protein diet because much of the food is not digested and is turned into waste matter. If you have several dogs, diet quality becomes an important issue not only in your pets' health, but also in the amount of yard cleanup you have to do. The more fiber in your pet's diet, the more poop you will have to scoop.

Vitamins

Good health depends on a balanced vitamin intake in the diet. Depending on how vitamins are absorbed and excreted by the body, they are classified as fat-soluble (vitamins A, D, E, and K) or water-soluble (all the B vitamins and vitamin C). Dogs are capable of making their own vitamin C and do not require supplementation in their diet (unlike

Supplements

If you feed Lotus a high-quality dog food, nutritional supplementation is most likely unnecessary. In fact, by supplementing his diet with other products, you may disrupt the nutritional balance you are striving to provide. Consult your veterinarian about any form of supplementation before adding it to Lotus's nutritional program.

humans, nonhuman primates, guinea pigs, and some fruit bats that develop scurvy and die without dietary vitamin C).

Vitamins must be correctly balanced in a dog's diet. An overdose of vitamins is just as dangerous as a vitamin deficiency. Excess vitamin intake, or a vitamin deficiency, can both cause serious medical problems.

Minerals

Minerals are necessary for life-sustaining activities that take place in the body every day. Minerals are required for skeletal growth and development and muscle and nerve function. Among the minerals required for life are calcium, phosphorus, sodium, potassium, magnesium, zinc, selenium, iron, manganese, copper, and iodine.

Like vitamins, minerals should be provided in a balanced ratio. Excessive supplementation of minerals can lead to serious medical conditions.

Additives and Preservatives

Additives and preservatives are substances added to the dog food to

Weigh your Shih Tzu regularly to make sure it is the proper weight for its age.

guidelines are provided on the dog food label, but the suggested amount per feeding may be more than Lotus requires. Just as you would not eat the same amount of food as your next-door neighbor, no two dogs are alike in their feeding requirements. Although there are all kinds of calculations you can do to determine Lotus's energy requirements and caloric intake, they probably will vary weekly, and possibly daily, especially if he is a young, active, growing puppy.

The amount you feed Lotus also depends on the quality of the food you provide. If you feed a high-quality dog food that is easily digested, a smaller amount is needed than if you feed a mediocre diet filled with bulk and fiber material that cannot be digested. You will also notice that Lotus will produce less fecal material when fed a quality diet, because most of the food is used for energy and less is going to waste.

The best way to know if Lotus is eating the proper amount is to check his overall physical condition. *You should be able to feel the ribs, but not see them.* Weigh him once a week, if possible, and not less than once a month. You can do this by holding Lotus and weighing both of you on a bathroom scale, then weighing yourself alone. Subtract your weight from the combined weight and the difference is Lotus's weight. Another option is to ask your veterinarian if you can use the hospital walk-on platform scale each week. If you notice any weight loss

improve or enhance color, flavor, and texture, and to extend product shelf life. Additives, such as antioxidants, are added to dog food to help keep fat in the food from becoming rancid over time. Other additives are used to slow down bacterial and fungal growth.

How Much to Feed

As mentioned earlier, nutritional needs vary according to the stage of development, activity level, and environmental conditions. Basic feeding or gain, your veterinarian can advise you if Lotus is within the appropriate weight range and whether to change the diet or meal size. Remember that an adult Shih Tzu weighs 9 to 16 pounds (4 to 7.2 kg), so don't let Lotus become too heavy.

When to Feed

Shih Tzu puppies are active individuals that burn off calories quickly. Their initial growth phase is during the first six months of life, although technically they are still puppies until eight to twelve months of age, or when they reach puberty. While Lotus is a puppy, he should be fed at least four times a day because he has a small stomach and a high metabolism. As a general guideline, when his growth and development begin to slow down, you can decrease the feeding schedule to three meals (at about twelve weeks of age), and later two meals (at about six months of age) a day. Be sure to consult your veterinarian to be certain this feeding schedule matches Lotus's specific needs.

Unless Lotus is a very active dog, he probably will not require more than one to two meals a day when he is an adult. Ideally the meals should be provided at twelve-hour intervals, or if only one meal is provided, in the early evening, after he has exercised and before bedtime. If all of the food has not been eaten after twenty minutes, remove it. An after-dinner leisurely stroll before bedtime will help Lotus sleep more comfortably.

Some people prefer to feed free choice (also called "free feed" or *ad libitum*), which means that food is available at all times and the dog eats whenever it desires. This method works well for dogs that are nibblers, not gluttons. Although free-choice feeding is convenient, it is difficult to know exactly how much food Lotus is eating daily. It also is not usually successful because most dogs will eat even if they are not hungry. These gourmands eventually will exceed their ideal weight if food is not limited.

Puppies are playful and active and they burn off calories quickly. They need several feedings daily.

Obesity

Obesity is a form of malnutrition in which there is a ratio of too much fat to lean body tissue. We usually think of malnutrition as being a shortage of food, resulting in a thin, starving individual. However, malnutrition means bad nutrition (from the French word "mal" for "bad"). Malnutrition refers to all aspects of unbalanced nutrition, whether it is too little or too much.

Obesity in dogs has now reached epidemic proportions in the United States—more than 30 percent of the canine population is obese. Overfeeding (especially overfeeding a puppy or adolescent) and inactivity can cause obesity, which in turn can lead to heart disease, skeletal and joint problems (such as arthritis), and metabolic diseases (such as diabetes).

The most effective way to prevent Lotus from becoming overweight is to closely monitor his food intake and not overfeed him. *Overeating is the most common cause of obesity in dogs.*

Water

Water is the most important of all nutrients. Water is necessary for life because it is needed for digestion, to metabolize energy, and to eliminate waste products from the body. Although you would never deprive Lotus of food, he could survive longer without food than without water. A 10 percent body water loss can result in death, and water makes up more than 70 percent of your dog's lean adult body weight.

Dogs lose body water throughout the day, in the urine and feces, by evaporation, panting, drooling, and

Begging for food is a bad habit. To prevent begging, don't allow your Shih Tzu in the kitchen or dining area during mealtimes and, if your pet begs, ignore it. This will help prevent obesity.

No Begging, Please!

Two important rules:

1. Teach your Shih Tzu not to beg.

2. If your pet begs, ignore him, no matter how cute he looks.

This is the best way you can avoid overfeeding your pet and prevent obesity.

footpad sweating. Water depletion occurs more rapidly in warm or hot weather or when an animal is active. Body water must be replaced continually, so it is extremely important that fresh water be available at all times to avoid dehydration and illness. It is also very important that you do not leave Lotus outside in hot weather. Shih Tzus cannot tolerate hot weather.

It is important to monitor how much water Lotus drinks each day. If he seems to be continually thirsty or to drink more than usual, it could be a warning sign for possible illness, such as diabetes or kidney (renal) disease. If he is not drinking as much as he should, he can become dehydrated and develop a medical condition. Adequate water intake is especially important in older animals, because they may have impaired kidney function. If you think Lotus is drinking too much, or not drinking enough, contact your veterinarian right away. It might be a sign of a serious health problem.

Food Myths

There are some common food myths about the effects of various foods in the canine diet. Garlic is often credited with killing worms and repelling fleas. Brewer's yeast and onions also have been touted as flea repellents. Unfortunately, these foods have no action against internal or external parasites, although dogs can benefit from the B vitamins in Brewer's yeast. Onions, on the other hand, can cause toxicity in dogs and are not recommended in the diet.

Food Allergies

Just like people, dogs can develop allergies to certain foods. For example, some dogs are sensitive to corn (a major ingredient in many commercial dog foods) or corn oil, or beef in the diet.

Food allergies often are noted for their effect on the animal's skin and coat. Food allergies can cause itchy, reddened skin and hair loss. In more severe cases, hair loss and sore spots can extend to the feet, legs, face, and ears.

If Lotus is scratching his skin excessively for no apparent reason, and his coat does not look its best, ask your veterinarian if a change to a hypoallergenic diet would be beneficial.

Note: Use stainless steel food dishes. Plastic or hard rubber dishes can cause skin allergies (contact dermatitis) in some animals.

Developing Good Eating Habits

• Never allow Lotus to beg. If he does, ignore him. If you can't ignore his pleading eyes, put him in another room where you don't have to see them. Be firm about the "no begging" rule and be consistent!

Your Shih Tzu may be an eager eater. Be careful not to overfeed your pet.

• Designate a place for the dog food bowl and put everything Lotus is to eat in the bowl. This will discourage him from begging food from your hands or from the dinner table.

• Feed on a regular schedule and feed enough to satisfy Lotus's caloric needs.

• Do not feed Lotus any food intended for humans, especially snack foods and candies. The high sugar and salt content in junk "people food" is as bad for dogs as it is for humans.

• Do not feed meat, fish, poultry, or eggs raw. These products can be contaminated with *Salmonella*, *E. coli*, or other bacterial pathogens that can cause fatal illness.

• Do not feed bones. They can splinter and become lodged in the throat or gastrointestinal tract.

• Determine in advance which food treats, and how many, Lotus will be allowed each day. Do not exceed the limit you have set.

• Feed snacks and treats primarily as training rewards or special praise.

• Teach children not to feed meals or give treats to Lotus without your permission.

• Do not allow Lotus in the kitchen while you are preparing food, or in the dining room during family mealtime. This prevents begging.

Chapter Eight

Keeping Your Shih Tzu Healthy

It's hard to believe that not so long ago, we had no way to prevent or treat most canine health problems. It was common for dogs to die from a wide variety of health problems including malnutrition, severe parasitism, and bacterial and viral diseases. Today's Shih Tzu is a lucky dog indeed, benefiting from all the medical advances, prescription products, good nutrition, and creature comforts that people enjoy.

Veterinarians today have received many years of training in medicine and surgery, and many veterinary clinics are subject to inspection and accreditation. If Cookie requires medical expertise in a specific area, board-certified veterinary specialists are available to help.

It is reassuring to know so many resources are available if they are ever needed, but *the best way to keep your pet healthy is to avoid or prevent problems before they start*. Preventive health care is the most important care you can give your dog. It includes regular physical examinations, vaccinations against disease, an effective parasite control program, correct nutrition (see Feeding Your Shih Tzu, Chapter Seven), regular exercise, good dental care, routine grooming (see Grooming Your Shih Tzu, Chapter Six), and plenty of love and attention for her physical and emotional well-being.

Selecting a Veterinarian

You and your veterinarian will be partners sharing responsibility for ensuring your companion's health throughout her life. For this reason, you should be as particular about choosing Cookie's veterinarian as you are about your own doctor. Fortunately, there is no shortage of excellent veterinarians, but how do you find the veterinarian who's just right for you and Cookie? Here are some guidelines to help you in the selection process:

1. Ideally, you should try to find a veterinarian who appreciates Shih Tzus as much as you do and who is familiar with the breed's special characteristics and needs. Start

Your Shih Tzu is a lucky dog. Specialized veterinary services and new vaccines and medications are available to improve your pet's quality of life. Find a veterinarian for your companion before you need one.

looking for a veterinarian before you need one.

2. Ask satisfied Shih Tzu owners and members of the local kennel clubs which veterinarians they recommend in your area. Word of mouth is one of the best ways to find a veterinarian. Many veterinarians advertise in telephone directories, but the size or style of an advertisement is not an indicator of the best match for your requirements.

3. Consider convenience. What are the doctors' office hours, schedule, and availability? Who is available on weekends and holidays, or in case of emergency? How close is the veterinary clinic or hospital? Will you be able to travel there within a reasonable amount of time in the event of an emergency?

4. Is there a consistency of personnel and continuity of communication? The veterinary support staff will play an important role in Cookie's health care. Have the veterinary technicians (animal health care nurses) received formal certified training and are they licensed as registered veterinary technicians?

5. What are the fees for services? Most veterinarians provide a price estimate for anticipated services and expect payment when service is rendered. Be sure to ask what types of payment methods are available.

6. Request an appointment to tour the veterinary hospital facilities. Examine all of the hospital during your tour, particularly its cleanliness and odors, the surgical suites and isolation wards, and the availability of monitoring equipment for surgery and anesthesia.

You and your veterinarian will develop a relationship of mutual respect and trust. You will rely on each other for accurate information and work together as a team. The chemistry among you, your veterinarian, and Cookie should be just right.

Preventive Health Care

Physical Examinations

You know your companion better than anyone. You know when Cookie is happy and feeling great and you will be the first to notice if she is not

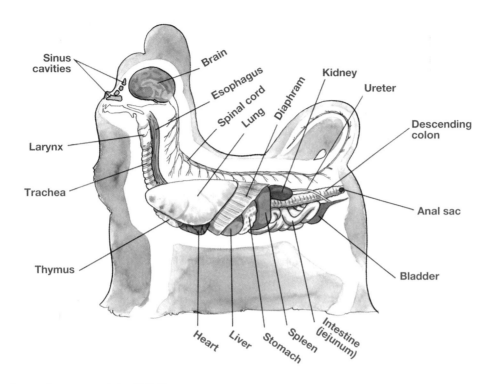

Internal anatomy of the Shih Tzu.

acting like herself, seems depressed, doesn't want to eat, is limping, loses weight, or has any other problems. Of course, in these cases you would call your veterinarian to schedule an appointment for a physical examination, diagnosis, and treatment. However, the more you know about Cookie's condition and the sooner you recognize any potential problems, the more you can help her—and your veterinarian.

A home physical examination is a good way to detect a possible problem before it becomes serious. The home examination is not a replacement for the veterinary examination, but it gives you a good idea of your dog's health condition. If you notice something wrong with Cookie, call your veterinarian right away and describe your observations and concerns. Keep a record of Cookie's condition, noting the date and the time. Add information to the record if there are any changes. This information will be useful in assessing the progression or improvement of a condition over time.

To detect illness in an animal, you must first be able to recognize normal appearance, attitude, stance,

Those expressive eyes should always be bright and clear. If your pet has any eye problems, contact your veterinarian right away.

abdominal pain. A drooping head may mean neck pain. A tilted head could indicate ear pain, ear infection, parasites in the ear, or a nervous system problem.

3. Now watch Cookie's movement and gaits. Does she walk, trot, and run willingly and normally, or does she move with difficulty, or limp? This might be hard to determine because Shih Tzus have short legs covered with lots of hair and they move very quickly.

4. Does Cookie seem to experience pain when you handle her feet or legs? The origin of lameness is often difficult to detect, especially if the dog is lame in more than one limb. Lameness could be due to injury, joint problems, muscular or skeletal problems, or nervous system problems. Often, lameness is due to a foreign object, like a thorn in the footpad or a grass awn lodged between the toes, so be sure to check all four of Cookie's feet.

5. Now look at Cookie up close, from the nose to the toes. And yes, a cold, wet nose is normal for a dog, although a dry nose does not necessarily mean she is sick. The nose should be free of discharge (thick mucus or pus), but it is not unusual for dirt to lodge in the little "corner grooves" of her nose (the nares). This can be cleaned away gently with a soft tissue or cotton-tipped swab and warm water. If the nares become sore or raw, you can spread a thin layer of Vaseline or Aquaphor over the area, taking care not to plug the small, sometimes pinched, nasal

movement, and behavior. Here are a few things to look for when you examine your Shih Tzu:

1. First, watch Cookie from a distance. Does she have a happy attitude and does she appear to be in good condition? Is her coat healthy? Is she well proportioned (not too thin, not too heavy)? Do you see anything unusual?

2. Observe Cookie while she stands. Does she stand naturally and place her weight on all four feet, or is she favoring one foot? If her back is hunched up, she may have back or passages. Frequent applications are usually necessary because dogs usually lick off medication on the nose shortly after it is applied.

6. Check Cookie's eyes. They should be bright and clear. If any mucus has accumulated around the eyes, gently remove it with a soft, clean tissue. If you see signs of squinting, redness, or infection (green or yellow discharge) in or around the eyes, or if the colored part of the eye (the iris) or surface of the eye (cornea) appear cloudy or hazy, contact your veterinarian immediately. These are signs of serious and painful eye problems that can quickly lead to loss of vision and sometimes loss of the eye itself. Keep hair cleared away from the eyes to prevent irritation and excessive tearing.

7. Look inside Cookie's mouth. Are the gums bright pink? Are the teeth free of tartar accumulation, or do they need to be cleaned and polished? Does Cookie have bad breath? More than 85 percent of adult dogs suffer from some degree of periodontal disease and this can cause bad breath. Periodontal disease is very common in small breeds, including the Shih Tzu. Sometimes certain odors detected in bad breath indicate a metabolic problem, such as ketosis.

8. Look inside Cookie's ears. Shih Tzus frequently need to have their ears cleaned to prevent the ear canal from becoming moist, thickened, and matted with wax. If Cookie's ears are overly sensitive, red, or have a foul odor, contact your veterinarian immediately for medical treatment. If she shakes her head or scratches at her ears, it could mean she has an ear infection, a foreign body, or parasites, such as ear mites.

9. Now look at Cookie's hair and skin. Is the skin healthy, or is it dry and flaky, or greasy? Is there evidence of parasitism, such as fleas or ticks?

10. Take your pet's pulse. You can do this by simply pressing your fingers against the inside middle portion of her upper thigh. Normal heart rate will range between 80 and 140 beats per minute, depending on whether she is at rest or has just been very active.

11. If Cookie has not been spayed, check her regularly for signs of estrus. You don't want to leave her within reach of unwanted suitors during her estrous cycle. Check her nipples for signs of lumps and bumps that could be mammary

Observe your pet's gait, or movement, closely for signs of lameness.

(breast) cancer. If you have an intact male (not neutered), both of his testicles should be fully descended into the scrotum. If one or both testicles are missing, give your veterinarian a call. Retained testicles may be an inherited problem. If the retained testicle is not surgically removed, it can become cancerous in later life. Check for any discharge at the end of the penis or sheath. Some discharge from the sheath is common and considered normal for many dogs, especially intact males. Treatment is not usually necessary, nor is it often effective. However, if there is an excessive amount of discharge from the sheath, this could indicate a medical problem.

12. Finally, check under the tail for signs of problems such as swelling, hernias, anal gland problems, cysts, inflammation, diarrhea, and parasites (tapeworms).

Make a Movie on Movement

Does your Shih Tzu move correctly? It's easier to judge with the help of modern technology. Take a camcorder and record your Shih Tzu as she walks on a level surface toward you, away from you, from left to right, and right to left. Try to record your pet in relationship to a straight, stationary object, such as a low, even fence or hedge.

Now play your recording back in slow motion or frame by frame. It's amazing what you will see! This is a great technique for judging movement of animals in the show ring. It is also very helpful if you think your pet is lame. Watch for head-bobbing. A dog's head will drop lower when weight is placed on the sound foot. The head will lift up as the sore foot or leg is forced to bear weight. The animal's topline (back) will appear to rise and fall and not stay even in relationship to the horizontal fence in the background.

This is a simple but excellent method to detect problems in movement that are not immediately obvious or that are hidden by a long coat and very fast legs!

Vaccinations

Vaccinations (inoculations, immunizations) are the best method currently available to protect Cookie against serious, life-threatening diseases. Although you will do your best to prevent her from coming into contact with sick animals, at some time your companion will be exposed to germs that cause illness, whether you know it or not. Anywhere you take her—parks, rest stops, campgrounds, dog shows, obedience classes, or your veterinarian's office—Cookie might be exposed to viruses and bacteria that could cause severe disease and possibly death. You can also bring home infectious material on your shoes and clothing. Although there is not a vaccine available for every known canine disease, we do have vaccines for the most common and deadly diseases. No vaccine is 100 percent guaranteed effective; however, if you are conscientious about Cookie's health and vaccination schedule, you can rest assured she has a very good chance of being protected against serious illness.

You will note that veterinarians may recommend different vaccination schedules. This is because *vaccinations should be a medical decision, not a calendar event.* In other words, the type of vaccination and when it is administered should be appropriate to your Shih Tzu's lifestyle, age, health condition, past medical history, and potential risk of exposure. Another reason vaccination schedules may vary is that most vaccine label recommendations are based on historical precedent. For example, it has been found that by vaccinating large populations of animals annually, there has been a decline in disease incidence in the overall canine population. However, it has not yet been scientifically demonstrated that vaccinations must be given every year. In fact, vaccines vary in range of purity, potency, safety, and efficacy. Vaccination is a potent medical procedure with profound impact. There are significant benefits, as well as some risks, associated with any vaccine. Vaccine administration should always take into consideration the animal's risk of exposure (population density), susceptibility or resistance to disease,

Normal Shih Tzu Temperature

Normal body temperature for a Shih Tzu ranges from 99.5 to 102.5°F (37.5 to 39°C). A very excited dog may have an elevated temperature as high as 103.5°F, but it should not exceed this value.

To take your pet's temperature, lubricate the tip of the thermometer with Vaseline or Aquaphor and gently insert it approximately 2 inches (5 cm) into the rectum and hold onto the end of the thermometer. Wait two minutes, or, if you are using a digital thermometer (preferable), wait for the beep, then check the temperature reading. Ear thermometers, such as those used for children, may also be used.

No two animals are alike. Vaccine schedules and the vaccines to be used should be determined according to each animal's individual situation. Age, health, and risk of disease exposure must be carefully considered.

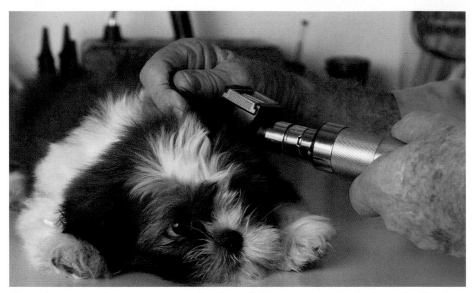

From the nose to the toes, your veterinarian will do a complete physical examination to make sure your pet is in excellent health.

and overall health (nutrition, parasites, age, special medical conditions).

The Debate over Vaccinations

Vaccinations, when to give them, and how often to booster them, are all topics of hot debate in the veterinary community. Recently the American Veterinary Medical Association and the American Animal Hospital Association have changed some of their earlier recommendations, and there is not total agreement among veterinarians about which vaccines to give and how often to give them. It has been frequently suggested that some vaccines need to be given only during puppyhood, followed by a series of boosters, and that annual revaccination for life is unnecessary, possibly

even potentially harmful. Other veterinarians are concerned that if vaccines are given too early in life, they may interfere with a dog's immune system or cause problems later in life.

Many veterinarians recommend measuring blood titers of antigens against specific diseases before giving a booster immunization. The thinking is that if the titer is high enough, the dog may have enough protection against the disease and not require a booster shot. Unfortunately, the level of antigens does not always correlate with the degree of immunity an animal has against disease, and some antigen levels are caused by disease exposure, rather than immunity due to vaccination. Clearly, more study needs to be done regarding vaccine efficacy, safety,

Vaccination Schedule for Puppies

Vaccine	Age for First Inoculation	Age for Second Inoculation	Age for Third Inoculation
Distemper	8 weeks	12 weeks	16 weeks
Hepatitis	8 weeks	12 weeks	16 weeks
Parvovirus*	8 weeks	12 weeks	16 weeks
Parainfluenza	8 weeks	12 weeks	16 weeks
Leptospirosis**	12 weeks	16 weeks	
Bordetella	12 weeks	16 weeks	
Lyme Disease***	12 weeks	16 weeks	
Coronavirus**	8 weeks	12 weeks	
Rabies****	12 weeks	15 months	

*Some veterinarians recommend a fourth parvovirus vaccination at 20 weeks of age because many animals do not develop sufficient immunity against this disease before five months of age.

**Leptospirosis and coronavirus vaccination may not be necessary or recommended. Consult your veterinarian.

***Check with your veterinarian to see if Lyme disease is a problem in your area or in any areas in which you will be traveling with your pet.

****Rabies vaccination intervals vary according to state laws and the type of vaccines used. Consult your veterinarian.

Note: Adult booster vaccinations should be given as recommended by your veterinarian based on your dog's health and specific requirements.

long-term effects, and the correlation between antigen titers and immunity.

Obtaining Vaccines

Some pet owners purchase vaccines on-line or from pet stores or feed stores. The problem with some of these vaccines is that there is no quality assurance and the care of the product is unknown. Vaccines must be prepared properly and stored at the correct temperatures. For example, if a vaccine that requires constant refrigeration is allowed to become warm, it will be ineffective. It may be shipped to you with a cold pack and arrive cold, but you cannot be sure that it was kept cold since the time of manufacture. In addition, there are some clinical conditions in which an animal should not be vaccinated. The owner may not be aware of the condition or restrictions for the use of a specific vaccine.

Common Canine Diseases

Distemper

Cause: Viral.

Spread: Airborne; body excretions.

Contagion: Highly contagious, especially among young dogs.

Symptoms: Respiratory: difficulty breathing; coughing; discharge from nose and eyes. *Gastrointestinal:* vomiting, diarrhea, dehydration. *Nervous:* trembling, blindness, paralysis, seizures. *Skin:* pustules on skin; hard footpads.

Treatment: None. Supportive therapy only; antibiotics to prevent secondary bacterial infection.

Parvovirus

Cause: Viral.

Spread: Contaminated feces.

Contagion: Highly contagious, especially among puppies.

Symptoms: Gastrointestinal: diarrhea, dehydration, vomiting. *Cardiac:* heart problems and heart failure.

Treatment: None. Supportive therapy only; antibiotics to prevent secondary bacterial infection.

Infectious Canine Hepatitis

Cause: Viral.

Spread: Body excretions, urine.

Contagion: Highly contagious, especially among puppies and young dogs.

Symptoms: Liver: inflammation, jaundice. *Eyes:* "blue eye" due to inflammation and fluid buildup. *Kidney:* damage, pain, and internal bleeding.

Treatment: None. Supportive therapy only; antibiotics to prevent secondary bacterial infection.

Leptospirosis

Cause: Bacterial.

Spread: Urine contaminated in kennels or from wild animals.

Contagion: Highly contagious.

Symptoms: Kidney: damage and failure. *Liver:* damage and jaundice, internal bleeding, anemia.

Treatment: Antibiotics.

Common Canine Diseases (continued)

Parainfluenza and Bordetellosis (Both cause "kennel cough.")

Cause: Viral (Parainfluenza). Bacterial (Bordetellosis).

Spread: Airborne, sneeze and cough droplets.

Contagion: Highly contagious, especially in boarding kennels and dog shows.

Symptoms: Respiratory: dry, hacking, continual cough of several weeks' duration that may cause permanent damage to airways.

Treatment: Supportive therapy; antibiotics; cough suppressants.

Coronavirus

Cause: Viral.

Spread: Feces.

Contagion: Highly contagious.

Symptoms: Gastrointestinal symptoms: vomiting, diarrhea, dehydration.

Treatment: None. Supportive therapy only; antibiotics to prevent secondary bacterial infection.

Lyme Disease

Cause: Bacterial.

Spread: Spread by the bite of an infected tick or contaminated body fluids.

Symptoms: Swollen lymph nodes, lethargy, loss of appetite, joint swelling, lameness; can induce heart and kidney disease.

Treatment: Supportive therapy; antibiotics.

Rabies

Cause: Viral.

Spread: Saliva (bite wounds).

Symptoms: Fatal, preceded by nervous system signs including paralysis, incoordination, and change in behavior.

Treatment: None (postexposure treatment does exist for humans).

Vaccination Schedules

The type of vaccines to give and when to give them should be a decision made carefully by you and your veterinarian, with consideration of your pet's risk of exposure to disease and the need for protection. For these reasons, *the preceding vaccination schedule should be considered only as a guideline*. You and your veterinarian will discuss and determine Cookie's individual vaccination program depending on her needs and health at the time of examination.

Parasite Control

Giant strides have been made in recent years regarding parasite control, both internal (roundworms, hookworms, whipworms, tapeworms, heartworms, and protozoa) and external (fleas, ticks, and mange-causing mites). Many products used in the past have been replaced by recent, convenient parasiticides. For example, prevention and treatment of internal parasites, heartworm prevention, and treatment for flea infestation can be made possible by giving your dog a single tablet monthly. There are products that can be applied topically once a month; just a few drops can kill external parasites.

With such a wide variety of new and effective pharmaceuticals available to prevent and treat internal and external parasites, there is no reason why any dog should be tormented or made sick by parasites. These products are available from your veterinarian and require a physical examination, a heartworm test, and fecal examination before they can be dispensed.

Internal Parasites

Internal parasites, such as worms and protozoa, can have a serious impact on a dog's health. They can cause diarrhea, and in severe cases dehydration and malnutrition. In addition, many internal parasites of dogs are transmitted through contact with feces and can pose a serious health threat to people, especially children. This is why it is important to keep Cookie in a clean environment and to teach children to wash their hands before eating or after handling any dog.

For all of the internal and external parasites, there is now a wide variety of medications called parasiticides available that kill both internal and external parasites. Many of these

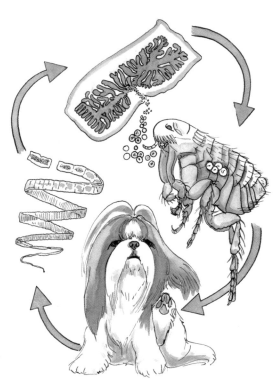

Life cycle of the tapeworm.

Internal Parasites

Roundworms

Mode of Transmission to Dogs: Ingestion of eggs in feces of infected animals; transmitted from mother to pup in utero or in the milk.

Mode of Transmission to Humans: Accidental ingestion of eggs from contact with infected fecal material.

Prevention: Parasiticides should be administered to pups as early as three weeks of age and should be repeated regularly as necessary.

Hookworms

Mode of Transmission to Dogs: Ingestion of larvae in feces of infected animals; direct skin contact with larvae.

Mode of Transmission to Humans: Direct skin contact with larvae in soil contaminated with feces of infected animals; accidental ingestion of larvae.

Prevention: Parasiticides.

Whipworms

Mode of Transmission to Dogs: Contact with feces.

Mode of Transmission to Humans: None.

Prevention: Parasiticides.

Tapeworms

Mode of Transmission to Dogs: Contact with fleas and feces; ingestion of fleas; eating raw meat (wild rodents, road-kills).

Mode of Transmission to Humans: Accidental ingestion of larvae.

Prevention: Parasiticides.

Heartworms

Mode of Transmission to Dogs: Mosquito bite.

Mode of Transmission to Humans: None.

Prevention: Parasiticides.

Protozoa

Mode of Transmission to Dogs: Contact with feces.

Mode of Transmission to Humans: Accidental ingestion of organisms in fecal material.

Prevention: Parasiticides.

External Parasites

Fleas

Animal Health Problems: Allergy to flea saliva; skin irritation and itching; transmission of tapeworms.

Contagion to Humans: Fleas may bite humans. Tapeworms also may be indirectly transmitted to people.

Ticks

Animal Health Problems: Transmission of Lyme disease; skin irritation and infection.

Contagion to Humans: Humans can contract Lyme disease from direct contact with ticks. Always wear gloves when removing ticks from your dog to avoid contracting the disease.

Sarcoptic mange

Animal Health Problems: Skin lesions and itching; hair loss.

Contagion to Humans: Sarcoptic mange can spread from pets to people by contact.

Demodectic mange

Animal Health Problems: Skin lesions; localized or generalized hair loss.

Contagion to Humans: No.

products can be given once a month on a regular basis.

Signs of Illness

If you have to ask yourself whether you should call your veterinarian, then it's a safe bet that you should; if Cookie was looking and acting completely healthy and normal, you wouldn't be asking yourself that question. Better to be safe and contact your veterinarian if you think your pet is having a problem. Treating the condition at its very onset can make all the difference between rapid recovery and prolonged illness.

After conducting a physical examination on your companion, contact your veterinarian to discuss any abnormal or unusual findings.

Some abnormal findings may not be an illness in and of themselves (such as loss of appetite or listlessness), but they are good indicators that Cookie is experiencing other medical problems that require veteri-

Cats are often a source of flea infestation for dogs.

nary attention. Contact your veterinarian if Cookie is having any of the following problems:
- Fever
- Pain
- Loss of appetite
- Lethargy
- Vomiting
- Diarrhea
- Discharge from the eyes
- Coughing
- Sneezing
- Wheezing
- Difficulty breathing
- Difficulty swallowing
- Choking
- Limping
- Head shaking
- Trembling
- Blood in the urine or stools
- Inability to urinate
- Inability to have a bowel movement
- Severe constipation
- Dehydration
- Weight loss

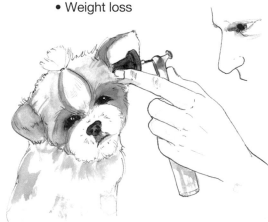

Ear problems can be painful. At every exam, your veterinarian will check your pet for ear infections, foreign objects, and parasites.

Selected Diseases and Conditions in Shih Tzus

Shih Tzus are strong, sturdy little dogs, but like every other breed of dog, or animal species for that matter, Shih Tzus can have problems. Each dog breed is predisposed to certain conditions or disorders. This does not mean that the problems are unique to a specific breed. Many dog breeds share the same health conditions. It also doesn't mean that your dog will ever experience any of these problems, or that it is widespread within the breed. It simply means that when there are problems, these are the types most commonly observed in the breed. So don't let this list of health considerations frighten you. Most likely, Cookie will not have any of these conditions, but if she does, this list will help you recognize them.

Brachycephalic conditions:
• Elongated soft palate
• Small or pinched nostrils
• Breathing difficulties
• Cleft lip, cleft palate
Eye problems:
• Lagophthalmos—inability to close the eyelids completely.
• Proptosis—eye forced out of the socket, usually by trauma. The eyelids close behind the eyeballs and shut off blood supply to the eyes. *This is an emergency that must be treated within minutes to prevent blindness. Take your Shih Tzu to your veterinarian immediately!*
• Distichiasis—abnormal position of eyelashes on the margin of the eyelids, causing the eyelashes to rub against and irritate the surface of the eye, leading to ulceration and scarring of the cornea and eventual blindness.
• Trichiasis—aberrant lashes growing inward from the conjunctival surface of the upper eyelid.
• Ectopia cilia—abnormal location of the eyelashes. Instead of growing out from the eyelid margins, the eyelashes grow out from the conjunc-

---

Windows to the Soul

Your Shih Tzu has big, beautiful, clear eyes that melt your heart. No wonder the eyes are called the "windows to the soul." Protect those fragile gems from injury, pain, and loss of vision. If you see your pet squinting or tearing, or if she has any discharge from the eyes, don't hesitate for a minute. *Contact your veterinarian immediately.* Eye problems are serious and usually very painful and if not treated right away can cause permanent loss of vision.

Eye problems can occur at any stage of life, and many conditions are hereditary.

All Shih Tzus should be checked annually by a board-certified veterinary ophthalmologist. Shih Tzus free of inherited eye problems should be certified by the Canine Eye Registration Foundation and rechecked annually.

tiva, usually from the center area of the upper eyelid. This is a painful condition that causes tearing and squinting.
• Third eyelid gland prolapse— "cherry eye."
• Entropion—inward rolling of the eyelids.
• Cataracts—clouding opacity of the lens of the eyes that may cause partial or total blindness.
• Keratitis—inflammation of the cornea (surface of the eye).
• Corneal ulcers—often associated with keratitis.
• Keratoconjunctivitis sicca "dry eye"—an abnormality of the composition of tears that causes corneal irritation, corneal ulceration, and blindness.
• Retinal detachment—the retina becomes separated from the back of the eye, leading to blindness.
• Progressive retinal atrophy (PRA)— degeneration of the cells of the retina; starts out as "night blindness" (difficulty seeing at night) and later develops into total blindness. PRA is an inherited disorder.
Dental abnormalities:
• Abnormal placement of teeth— misalignment, malocclusion.
• Abnormal number of teeth—missing teeth, retained deciduous (baby) teeth.
Ear conditions:
• Infections (due to a dropped ear that covers the ear canal and provides a warm, moist environment for bacteria and yeast to grow), characterized by a foul odor, waxy buildup, and scratching at the ears.

Shih Tzus love human companionship. If you must leave home for long periods of time, make arrangements for someone to keep your pet company.

Skin problems:
• Allergies—food, parasites (especially fleas).
• Immune-related skin problems.
• Endocrine (hormonal) conditions.
Bleeding disorders:
• Slow blood clotting time (Von Willebrand's disease).
Skeletal problems:
• Open fontanelle—failure of the "soft spot" on the skull to close completely by adulthood.
• Patellar luxation—the kneecap slips in and out of proper position due to a flaw in bone (femur) structure and weak ligaments. (This can be surgically corrected.)

Facts About Renal Dysplasia in Shih Tzus

1. Renal dysplasia is a failure of the kidneys to fully develop.

2. It is an inherited disorder in some Shih Tzus.

3. Kidney development usually stops around the time of birth.

4. Symptoms of the disease vary from severe to slight. Signs include excessive drinking and urinating, small size and weight, lethargy, lack of appetite, and overall poor condition.

5. Some animals with this condition die at an early age; others may live longer and slowly debilitate until they die.

6. Shih Tzus that are mildly affected may live a relatively normal life and pass the genetic condition on to their offspring.

7. Puppies produced from mildly affected parents can be more seriously affected than their parents.

8. Diagnosis is made by a kidney biopsy. Ultrasound imaging can detect the size and shape of the kidney and laboratory tests (blood urea nitrogen, creatinine, and urine specific gravity) can help determine how seriously a dog is affected.

9. There is now a DNA test to help identify Shih Tzus that are carrying this genetic disease.

10. All Shih Tzus should have a DNA test for renal dysplasia before they are used for breeding purposes.

11. Shih Tzus that have renal dysplasia or are carrying the genes for renal dysplasia should never be used for breeding purposes, in order to stop the spread of this inherited disorder within the breed.

12. Information and directions on DNA testing can be obtained from the American Shih Tzu Club (see Useful Literature and Web Sites, page 147).

• Achondroplasia—results in limb shortening and shortened maxilla (upper jaw) and is sometimes associated with patellar and elbow luxation.

Kidney (renal) problems:

• Stone formation in the kidneys or bladder.

• Renal dysplasia (a serious, common hereditary condition in the breed)—abnormal development, or incomplete development of the kidneys.

Liver problems:

• Portal systemic shunt is an abnormality in which embryonic blood vessel(s) that carried oxygenated blood from the placenta to the fetus does not close off within a few days of birth (as they should) and remain open. As a result, blood that would normally be directed to the liver for detoxification is shunted through the embryonic vessels and bypasses the liver. Hepatic (liver) detoxification is necessary to prevent accumulation in the body of toxic substances such as ammonia. Because the blood is shunted, toxins build up in the body causing a wide range of symptoms.

Signs of portal caval systemic shunt include chronic illness, urinary crystals and stones (ammonium biurate), increased thirst, weight loss, vomiting, diarrhea, salivation, and neurologic (nervous) symptoms. Affected animals may have seizures, circle aimlessly, press their heads against objects, or suffer from dementia.

Portal systemic shunt appears to be an inherited disorder in the Shih Tzu, and although it may be temporarily managed with a low-protein diet, the animal will eventually die of the disease unless the shunt is closed surgically. Surgery is difficult and delicate and not always successful.

If you think your Shih Tzu is suffering from portal systemic shunt, contact your veterinarian immediately. A surgical specialist may be required.

Animals with relatives known to be affected with portal shunt system should not be used for breeding.

First Aid for Your Shih Tzu

In spite of all your efforts to provide a safe environment for your Shih Tzu, accidents can happen, and many are life-threatening. The difference between life and death may depend on how prepared you are in an emergency situation. Be sure to have all your supplies on hand in advance so you do not waste precious time during an emergency trying to find what you need. As soon as possible, assemble a first aid emergency kit for

Cookie (see page 122). Set aside a special place for the kit. Keep your veterinarian's daytime and emergency telephone numbers near the phone and keep an additional copy of emergency telephone numbers in the first aid kit.

Supplies for Your Emergency First Aid Kit

There are some basic supplies and materials you need for your emergency first aid kit. These items are available from your veterinarian or local drugstore. You will no doubt think of additional things to include in the kit for the time when you are traveling or are away from home with

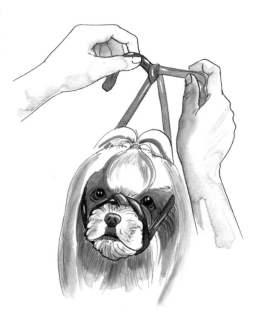

A muzzle will not hurt your pet and will not interfere with breathing. It will, however, protect you from being bitten if your dog is frightened or in pain.

First Aid Emergency Kit

Item	Purpose
Antihistamine	Treatment of allergic reaction to insect bites and stings.
Hydrogen peroxide 3 percent	To clean cuts and wounds; induce vomiting.
Povidone iodine solution	To clean and disinfect wounds.
Triple antibiotic ointment	Topical application to cuts and wounds.
Kaopectate	To treat diarrhea.
Milk of magnesia	To treat constipation.
Table salt	To induce vomiting.
Saline solution (sterile)	To flush and rinse wounds; can be used as an eyewash.
Eye lubricant or ointment (should *not* contain hydrocortisone)	To protect eyes in case of foreign body or injury until you can get treatment.

your pet. For example, bottled water, balanced electrolyte solution (Pedialyte), medication to prevent carsickness, tranquilizers, and painkillers (available from your veterinarian) are practical items to keep on hand.

Additional supplies:
• Bandage scissors
• Small, regular scissors
• Thermometer
• Tourniquet (an old necktie will work)
• Tweezers
• Forceps
• Mouth gag
• Cotton balls
• Q-tips
• Roll of gauze bandage
• Gauze pads (such as Telfa no-stick pads)
• Elastic bandage (preferably waterproof)
• Activated charcoal (in case of poisoning)
• Muzzle (an old necktie will work)
• Blanket (to provide warmth or to use as a stretcher)
• Paper towels
• Exam gloves (vinyl is preferable to latex because some people are allergic to latex)
• Flashlight

If you have not yet purchased a muzzle from the pet store, you can make a muzzle using an old necktie, rolled gauze, or a cloth strip about 18 inches (45 cm) long and 2 inches (5 cm) wide.

Wrap the gauze around the muzzle and mouth, making sure it does not pull on all the hair around the face, and tie it securely under the chin (this will not affect Cookie's ability to breathe). Be very careful not to close or block the nostrils. Cookie has a short muzzle, so take care not to tie the muzzle too close to her nose.

Take the ends of the gauze and tie them behind the head, on top of the neck. This muzzle will not hurt your pet and will protect you from being bitten. Make sure Cookie does not try to remove the muzzle with her front paws.

The goal of first aid treatment is to give Cookie whatever emergency care is required to save her life or reduce pain and suffering until you can contact your veterinarian. Before you begin any first aid treatment, the most important thing to remember is to protect yourself from being bitten or injured. Your usually loving pet may behave unpredictably when she is in pain or frightened. She may not recognize you or may instinctively lash out in self-defense at anyone who approaches her. If someone else is available, you can save time by having the person contact your veterinarian for advice while you begin emergency treatment. You may need assistance restraining Cookie while you treat her, so be sure the person you ask for assistance is experienced in animal handling. *Always muzzle your dog before initiating emergency treatment, for the safety of your pet and everyone involved.*

Bite Wounds

Bite wounds commonly result from encounters with other dogs, cats, or wild animals. Shih Tzus are not fighters, and because of their gentle, trusting nature they are, sadly, usually on the receiving end if another animal becomes aggressive.

In addition to thorough cleansing, antibiotic therapy is usually required to prevent bite wounds from becoming infected. If the wound is a tear, it may need to be sutured. If the injury is a puncture wound, it should be cleaned well with a disinfectant solution and allowed to remain open and drain. Look carefully through Cookie's coat. It is easy to miss a serious bite wound or injury under all the hair.

Be sure to consult your veterinarian immediately regarding any bite wound injuries and the type and dose of antibiotic necessary to prevent bacterial infection. In the unlikely event that a stray animal or a wild animal (raccoon, skunk, bat) has bitten Cookie, you need to discuss the possible risk of rabies with your veterinarian.

Bleeding

Bleeding can occur from injury, trauma, or serious health problems. The first thing you should do is firmly apply pressure over the wound to stop the bleeding. If you do not have gauze or a clean towel, any readily available, clean, absorbent material can be used as a compress. If a large blood vessel in a limb has been severed, it may be necessary to

If you think your pet does not feel well, contact your veterinarian immediately.

apply a tourniquet above the cut area. Be sure to loosen the tourniquet every 15 minutes to relieve pressure and allow circulation. Contact your veterinarian immediately.

Bone Fractures

Signs of bone fractures include swelling, pain and tenderness, abnormal limb position or movement, limping, and crepitation (crackling sensation when the area is touched). When bones are broken, they may remain under the skin or protrude up through the skin (open fracture).

If Cookie breaks a leg, and the bone is not exposed, you can make a temporary splint out of a small, flat piece of wood. First, muzzle your Shih Tzu, then gently tape the splint to the leg, allowing an overlap at each end of the break site. Do not wrap the splint to the leg so tightly that the paw swells, and do not wrap tape around the injury. If the bone is

exposed, do not try to replace it or cleanse it. Stop the bleeding and cover the wound with a sterile bandage. Make sure Cookie does not contaminate the open fracture by licking it. Contact your veterinarian immediately for advice. Cookie should receive veterinary care for the broken bone(s) as soon as possible, and definitely within 24 hours.

Breathing Difficulties

Shih Tzus' short noses and flat faces make it difficult for them to breathe as well as most other breeds of dogs. If the nostrils are pinched close together, the airways are even more narrow and breathing can become a chore. Shih Tzus may snort and snore and sound like they have the snuffles, but this can be normal for some individuals. Watch closely for signs of respiratory distress or infection. If your pet has any purulent (containing pus) nasal discharge (green or yellow discharge), contact your veterinarian immediately. An upper respiratory infection can quickly drop into the lungs and turn into pneumonia.

Some Shih Tzus have nostrils that are so occluded they must breathe through their mouths most of the time, especially when they are excited or active. Because of the shortened face, some Shih Tzus have an elongated soft palate that can block the trachea (air passageway to the lungs). When the soft palate covers the trachea, the animal struggles or gasps for air. If Cookie has this difficulty, try briefly covering her nose with your finger. This may help her force air out of the trachea, which in turn pushes the soft palate back into position so she can breathe again. Some Shih Tzus outgrow breathing difficulties as they age, but if your pet still has problems after her adult teeth are in place, contact your veterinarian. There are corrective surgical procedures that may help her, including opening her nostrils or shortening her soft palate.

Burns

Your Shih Tzu can suffer three kinds of burns:

1. Thermal burns—fire, boiling liquids, appliances

2. Electrical burns—chewing on electrical cords

3. Chemical burns—a variety of chemicals (such as corrosives, oxidizing agents, desiccants, and poisons)

If Cookie is burned, immediately cool the burn by applying a cold, wet

Take a Big Breath

Shih Tzus, like most brachycephalic breeds, can have trouble breathing, especially when they are hot, overexerted, or very excited. Here's what you can do to help your friend breathe a little easier:

• Do not take long walks or overexert your pet when it is hot outside.

• Do not allow your Shih Tzu to become stressed or overly excited.

• Use a harness instead of a collar for restraint and taking walks.

• Make sure your Shih Tzu always has plenty of cool, fresh water available.

• Keep your Shih Tzu out of areas where there is poor air quality due to dirt, dust, filth, sand, or pollen. All of these contaminants can make breathing difficult and can also damage the eyes.

• Ask your veterinarian if bronchodilators (or other medications that open airways and make breathing easier) would help your Shih Tzu.

cloth or an ice pack to the area. Protect the burned area from the air with an ointment (Neosporin or *aloe vera*). If she has suffered a chemical burn, immediately flush the burn thoroughly with water or saline to dilute and rinse the caustic chemical from the area.

Do not allow Cookie to lick the area or she will burn her mouth and

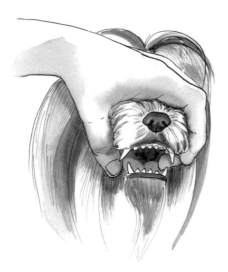

To give your Shih Tzu a tablet, open her mouth by grasping the muzzle and placing your thumb and index finger behind the upper canine teeth.

Place a finger of your opposite hand on the bottom jaw and press down while placing the tablet at the back of the mouth. Then close your pet's mouth so she can swallow. Make sure your Shih Tzu doesn't spit the tablet out when you're not looking!

esophagus with the substance. Contact your veterinarian immediately.

Choking

Choking occurs when an object (bone, food, toy, rock) becomes trapped, or lodged, in the mouth or throat. Because of your pet's facial and mouth structure, it's easy for her to choke on the most seemingly harmless object. If your pet starts to choke, she is in immediate danger of accidentally inhaling the foreign object. If the object obstructs the air passageway, Cookie will suffocate.

If your Shih Tzu is choking, you will need a good, clear view of her mouth and throat to see if the offending object can be found and safely removed. Shih Tzus have broad, but very small, jaws; therefore, it will be difficult to look into her mouth. A short wooden dowel 1–2 inches (2–4 cm) in diameter inserted between the back molars may serve as a gag to hold the mouth open while you use a flashlight to take a closer look down the throat. If you see the foreign object, be very careful not to push it further down the throat or into the trachea (windpipe). Remove the object with forceps when possible, to avoid being bitten. Contact your veterinarian immediately.

Cuts

Cuts should be shaved or clipped, cleansed well, and treated properly to prevent infection. Sometimes it is difficult to tell how deep the cut is, especially under all your pet's hair. Serious cuts may require sutures, so be sure to contact your veterinarian for advice. If the cut is not too deep, wash it with a mild soap and rinse it several times with water. Disinfect the injury with chlorhexidine solution or a mild soap. Dry the wound well and apply an antibiotic ointment to it.

Dystocia

Dystocia is the term used when a pregnant female has difficulty giving birth to her young. Dystocia occurs when the smooth muscles of the uterus become fatigued and weakened and can no longer contract. Dystocia also occurs when the uterus becomes twisted, or when the mother's pelvic area is abnormal or too small to allow passage of the puppy. In some cases, dystocia occurs because the puppy is too large or not in an appropriate birth position. (It is normal for puppies to be born either hindfeet and rump first or head first.)

Dystocia is a medical emergency that requires veterinary expertise. Medications to stimulate uterine contractions, or surgery, may be required to successfully deliver live pups. For this reason, it is a good idea to give your veterinarian advance notice of Cookie's delivery due date and make backup arrangements for emergency care if your veterinarian is unavailable the day she gives birth (whelps).

A good rule of thumb is to not allow Cookie to be in hard labor for more than two hours. If she has not whelped a pup within that time period, or if she has stopped labor altogether, she needs help. Contact your veterinarian immediately.

Heatstroke

Heatstroke is caused by exposure to high temperature and stress. Confinement in a car is one of the leading causes of heatstroke. On a hot day, a car parked in the shade, with the windows partially open, can still reach temperatures exceeding 120°F (48.9°C) within a few minutes. Overexertion on a hot day can also cause heatstroke. Dogs that are old or overweight are especially prone to heatstroke.

Signs of heatstroke include frantic, rapid breathing or struggling to breathe, panting, bright red gums and bright red curling tongue, thick drool, vomiting, diarrhea, dehydration, and a rectal temperature of 105 to 110°F (41 to 43°C). As the condition progresses, the body organs become affected, the animal weakens, goes into shock, then a coma, and dies. All of this can happen in a

If your Shih Tzu doesn't want her medicine, you might be able to disguise it by mixing it in some food. Warning: Shih Tzus are hard to fool!

very short period of time, and death can occur rapidly.

Shih Tzus do not tolerate heat and can quickly die of heatstroke. If Cookie is suffering from heatstroke, the first thing you must do is lower her body temperature. You can do this by placing her in a tub filled with cool *(not icy cold)* water. Be sure to keep Cookie's head above the water, especially if she is unconscious, so that she does not drown. Do not try to give her water to drink if she is unconscious. If a tub is unavailable, you can cool her by wetting her down with a garden hose if the water is cool. You can also wrap ice packs in a towel and place them near her body.

Heatstroke is a medical emergency that requires veterinary care. Cookie will need to be treated with intravenous fluids and various med-

Eye problems can be extremely painful and are common in Shih Tzus. If your pet has an eye problem, contact your veterinarian immediately. Failure to do so may rapidly lead to permanent loss of vision.

ications to treat shock and prevent cerebral edema (brain swelling). Even if she appears to be recovering, you must contact your veterinarian immediately for lifesaving follow-up care, especially if her temperature reaches 106°F (41.5°C) or more.

Eye Injuries

Eye injuries are extremely painful. The sooner you obtain treatment for Cookie's eyes, the sooner you can relieve your companion's pain and increase the chances of saving her eyes and vision. Injured eyes are very sensitive to the light, and exposure to even subdued lighting can hurt them. If Cookie's injury requires flushing and rinsing the eye, you can do this using a commercial eyewash solution or saline solution intended for use in the eyes. Place Cookie in a dark place and contact your veterinarian immediately. When you transport her to the hospital, place her in a travel crate and cover the crate with a blanket to keep out as much light as possible.

Insect Stings

If a bee stings Cookie, remove the stinger with tweezers (wasps and hornets do not leave their stingers). Try to gently remove the stinger without squeezing the base (where part of the bee's body is attached) so that additional venom is not injected into the site. This can be tricky, as the bee's stinger is barbed and the more you push on it, the deeper it penetrates.

Apply a paste mixture of water and baking soda or an ice pack to the area to relieve pain. An antihistamine may be necessary to prevent an allergic reaction to the sting, especially if Cookie is having difficulty breathing (ask your veterinarian for advice on an antihistamine and dose appropriate for your pet). You may also put a topical antihistamine cream around the stung area. Watch Cookie closely for the next two hours for signs of illness.

Most cases of stings from bees, hornets, and wasps are nothing more than painful annoyances. However, some animals develop a hypersensitivity to insect stings that can lead to anaphylactic shock and death. If the swelling worsens, or if Cookie becomes restless and has difficulty breathing, or starts to vomit, develops diarrhea, or loses consciousness, then contact your veterinarian immediately. This is a life-threatening situation and immediate professional treatment is necessary.

Poisoning

In addition to insect venom poisons, pets can be poisoned by eating or inhaling toxic substances, or by contact with poisons on their skin, mucus membranes, or eyes.

Signs of poisoning include restlessness, drooling, abdominal pain, vomiting, diarrhea, unconsciousness, seizures, shock, and death. Common sources of poison include rodent bait, certain houseplants, insecticides, medication overdose, spoiled food, antifreeze (ethylene glycol), and chocolate. (Chocolate contains theobromine, a substance similar to caffeine that is toxic to dogs.)

Be sure all the plants in your home and garden are nonpoisonous.

If Cookie has been poisoned, contact your veterinarian immediately for advice. If the poison came in a container (for example, antifreeze or rodent poison), read the container label and follow the emergency instructions for treating poisoning. If the instructions state that you should induce vomiting, you may accomplish this by giving Cookie 1/2 teaspoon of hydrogen peroxide 3 percent for every 10 pounds (4.5 kg) of body weight, or by tossing some table salt on the back of her tongue.

Activated charcoal is a good compound to use to dilute and adsorb ingested poisons. You can obtain activated charcoal in powder or tablet form from your veterinarian to keep in your first aid kit. If you do not have activated charcoal, and you do not have any products to induce vomiting, you can dilute the poison in the gastrointestinal tract by giving Cookie some milk. Do not try to give her any medication if she is unconscious.

The sooner the poisoning is diagnosed and treated, the better Cookie's chances of full recovery. Most poisonings require veterinary treatment in addition to the initial emergency care you provide. Contact your veterinarian immediately if you suspect that Cookie has been exposed to poison and, if it is available, take the box, bottle, or label of the product to your veterinarian.

Seizures

There are many causes of seizures, including epilepsy, poisoning, and brain trauma. Seizures may be mild or severe, ranging from a mild tremor of short duration to violent convulsions, chomping jaws and frothing at the mouth, stiffening of the neck and limbs, and cessation of breathing. During a severe seizure, a dog is not conscious and can be hurt thrashing about on the floor. Cookie may seem to be choking during a seizure, but avoid the temptation to handle her mouth, as you will be bitten. If her jaws clamp down on your fingers, they will not release until the seizure has ended. Simply try to prevent Cookie from injuring herself or hitting her head until the seizure has ended. After a seizure, Cookie will be exhausted and seem dazed. Place her in a quiet room with subdued light. Keep her comfortable and warm, and when she is conscious, offer her some water to drink.

Contact your veterinarian immediately for follow-up medical care and to determine the cause of the seizure and how to prevent another one from occurring.

Shock

Shock is a condition in which there is a decreased blood supply to vital organs and the body tissues die from inadequate energy supply. Blunt trauma (due to a fall, being stepped on, hit by a car, or kicked by a horse), blood loss, heatstroke, internal hemorrhage, blood loss from rodent bait poisoning (such as warfarin), bacterial toxins, and severe allergic reactions all can cause an animal to go into shock.

Shock is a serious emergency situation that results in a rapid death unless immediate veterinary care—including fluid and oxygen therapy and a variety of medications—are available. Signs of shock include extremely pale or blue mucous membranes (the gums should normally be bright pink), muscular weakness, staggering, vomiting, diarrhea, general weakness, difficulty breathing, increased heart rate, collapse, and coma.

Snakes, Toads, Lizards, and Spiders

Even a pampered housedog can encounter some danger, whether in the backyard or on a camping trip.

When your Shih Tzu plays in the yard, make sure she is safely confined and cannot reach fertilizers, yard sprays, chemicals, and pesticides.

Being aware of these potential problems can help you prepare in case of emergency.

Poisonous Snakebites

There are three groups of venomous snakes in North America:

1. The pit vipers, which include the rattlesnake, copperhead, and water moccasin (also known as the cottonmouth)

2. The coral snakes

3. The colubrids

The pit vipers and coral snakes are the most important. Rattlesnake bites occur most frequently in dogs in the West and Southwest, where rattlesnakes are common. The snake's bite produces painful, slitlike puncture wounds that rapidly become swollen. Common symptoms of snakebite include immediate severe pain, swelling, darkened tissue coloration, and tissue necrosis (tissue death).

Urgent, immediate veterinary attention is necessary. The lethality of the snakebite depends on the type of venom, its toxicity, the amount of venom injected, the size and health of the animal bitten, and how much time passes from the time the animal is bitten until it receives veterinary care. Because of its small size, a Shih Tzu can die rapidly from a snakebite if it is not treated immediately.

Poisonous snakebites require antivenin and antibiotic treatments. Even with treatment, the skin and underlying tissues may turn dark and slough off (rot) and leave serious scars.

The amount of venom injected (envenomization) cannot be determined simply by the appearance of the bite wound. The bite victim may become weak and exhibit various neurological signs, such as respiratory depression, and eventually go into shock and die.

If a venomous snake bites Cookie, keep her quiet and contact your veterinarian immediately. Your veterinarian may also recommend that you apply ice to the bite wound. Most veterinarians who practice in areas where snakebites are common keep antivenin available. All dogs bitten by venomous snakes should be hospitalized and monitored for at least 24 hours.

Note: Just as a note of general interest, for dogs that live outdoors in areas where rattlesnakes are a common problem, a new vaccine against

Shih Tzus love to participate in all family activities. During picnics or camp trips, remember that bees, wasps, snakes, and scorpions are more active and more likely to sting or bite in warm weather.

rattlesnake venom has recently been developed for use in dogs. Of course, Cookie lives indoors and should not be at great risk for snakebites, so unless there are special circumstances, it is highly unlikely your veterinarian would recommend this vaccine for her.

Toad Poisoning

Poisonous toads in the United States include the Colorado Rim toad and the marine toad. The most toxic toad varieties are located in the southwestern desert, the southeastern United States, and Hawaii. If you suspect that Cookie has come in contact with a poisonous toad, contact a veterinarian immediately.

Lizard Bites

The poisonous Gila monster lizard is found in the southwestern United States. It has grooved teeth (instead of fangs) with which it holds onto its victims. Most dogs are bitten on the upper lip. The Gila monster bite is extremely painful. No antivenin is available. Contact your veterinarian immediately for supportive treatment, antibiotics, and treatment to prevent shock.

Spiders

The brown spiders (fiddleback, brown recluse, and Arizona brown spider) all are found in the southern United States. There is no antidote available for their venomous bites. Black widow spiders are found throughout the United States. There is an antivenin available for black widow bites.

If Cookie is bitten by one of these spiders, take her to a veterinarian immediately for emergency care, antibiotic therapy, and antivenin therapy (for black widow spider bite).

The Senior Shih Tzu

With tender loving care, good nutrition, and a little luck, your Shih Tzu may live for 12 to 16 years or more. Just like people, some dogs age more slowly than others, especially those that have received good health care throughout their lives. As a general rule, a Shih Tzu is not quite a senior citizen until it reaches seven years of age. At this time, you may begin to notice changes beginning to take place in your pet's behavior, activity level, and physical stature. She may become arthritic, begin to slow down, and sleep more. She may develop problems with urination or bowel movements. Teeth and gums will require more attention due to accumulation of plaque and tartar on the teeth. The hair coat may become thinner, the skin less supple, and warts and other skin growths may appear. Cataracts become visible, hearing may diminish, and your friend will rely more on her sense of smell. These are all signs of the aging process.

As Cookie's body ages, it undergoes a slowing of metabolic rate that can lead to weight gain, a weaker heart and a reduction in kidney and

One of the nicest things you can do for your senior Shih Tzu is to give her a soft, comfortable bed and keep her warm.

liver function, general muscle weakening and atrophy, and a gradual deterioration in condition with a decreased resistance to diseases. Cookie may even show signs of disorientation or senility. All of these age-related changes, and the rate at which they occur, vary between individuals and are influenced by genetics, nutrition, environment, and the type of health care received in earlier years.

There are a number of things you can do to keep Cookie comfortable in her golden years.

1. Provide a soft, warm bed. Cold temperatures and hard surfaces make arthritis more painful.

2. Weigh Cookie monthly and do not allow her to become over- or underweight.

3. Take Cookie out regularly for easy, short walks on level, soft, nonslippery surfaces (such as grass). Keep her toenails trimmed.

4. Do not make Cookie jump up on furniture, climb stairs, or walk on slippery surfaces. Carry her when she needs to be carried.

5. Feed Cookie a diet appropriate for her age and health condition. An increase in protein quality and quantity recently has been demonstrated to be beneficial for some geriatric dogs, as well as having anticancer and antidiabetes effects.

6. Schedule physical examinations for Cookie every six months in her geriatric years. This will enable you to detect and address any age-related problems (such as cataracts or heart or kidney insufficiency) early. Remember that older dogs are more sensitive to anesthesia, especially if they are overweight.

7. If Cookie has failing eyesight or is hard of hearing, make every effort not to startle her. Speak to her reassuringly as you approach so she knows you are there, then touch her gently.

Euthanasia—When It's Time to Say Good-bye

Euthanasia means putting an animal to death humanely, peacefully, and painlessly. There are different ways in which veterinarians euthanize animals, depending on the circumstances. Euthanasia is usually done by first giving the animal a sedative to make it sleep deeply, then giving it a lethal substance by injection that ends its life almost instantly.

Even with the best care in the world, the sad day will come when you must consider euthanasia for your beloved companion. This understandably will be an emotionally painful time for you, because you will feel helpless in your inability to help your friend anymore; you will not want her to suffer for a moment, yet you cannot bear the thought of life without her. Nevertheless, if you begin to ask yourself whether your pet should be euthanized, there must be good reasons. The decision of when to euthanize is a difficult one that depends on many things; if suffering cannot be relieved, or if the quality of life is poor, or if the "bad days" simply outnumber the "good days," it is time to discuss euthanasia with your veterinarian. Your veterinarian can answer any specific questions you or your family may have. He or she also can help you if you wish to find a pet cemetery or desire cremation services.

During this emotional time, remember to take care of yourself and allow time to grieve. If you have children in the family, deal with the issue of animal loss at a level they can understand, comfort them, and let them share their grief. Take comfort in the knowledge that you took excellent care of your Shih Tzu throughout her life and that you made the best decisions regarding her health and welfare, even when you had to make the most difficult decision of all.

Chapter Nine
Training Your Shih Tzu

The Basics

To be an acceptable member of society, Lotus should first learn some basic manners. Because Shih Tzus are very bright and like to please, basic training should be fun, but don't forget that Shih Tzus are easily distracted and sometimes have a short attention span. They are easily excited and get bored after a few minutes. So keep training sessions brief and be patient. He will learn his lessons, as long as he stays focused.

The best way to hold Lotus's attention is to keep training sessions short, make them fun and interesting, and always end on a positive note. A small food reward now and then is a great incentive to Lotus to learn quickly and do the right thing. Don't give him a food reward every time he does something right—by keeping him guessing when the treat is coming, you will hold his attention longer. Besides, he should learn to do what he is asked because he *wants* to do it and because you will praise him and caress him when he does.

Training a Shih Tzu begins the moment you bring one home. It is never too early to start with simple, basic lessons. Studies have shown, for example, that leash training is easiest when a puppy is anywhere from five to nine weeks of age.

A basic puppy class, or dog training class, is the most effective way to begin obedience training and to teach Lotus to pay attention. There are as many different training techniques as there are dogs and trainers.

Dog training classes are a lot of fun. They are rewarding not only because your canine becomes a model citizen, but because you also will form many long-lasting friendships. Here are some training guidelines to get you started.

Commands

Come

Lotus first must learn his name so he can come when he is called and later respond to your commands. Start by calling his name when you feed him. It won't take him long to associate his name with a pleasant experience. In the beginning, you may also use small tidbits as a

It's never too early to start training your puppy. Just be sure training sessions are short and that they end on a positive note.

If you don't teach your Shih Tzu to stay off of the furniture, it will make itself comfortable wherever it wants.

reward, along with much praise, when he comes to you. Don't show him that you have a food reward. Keep him guessing. Over time, decrease the frequency of food rewards, but continue the praise. In no time at all, Lotus will come to you when called, purely for the attention you bestow on him, but that doesn't mean you can't still occasionally surprise him with a very small food reward!

Sit

The *sit* command is the easiest of all commands to teach your Shih Tzu. With some patience and consistency, Lotus will probably get the general idea and learn to sit (if even for a brief time) in one to three training sessions.

Start by holding a small piece of food over his nose and raising your hand over his head. As his head goes up to follow the tidbit, his hindquarters will naturally go down and you may apply gentle pressure on the rump to help him sit in the beginning. Give Lotus a tidbit reward as soon as he is seated.

The trick here is to keep Lotus from jumping up in his excitement to grab the treat from you. You may need to start over a few times, applying slight pressure on his rump to keep him in place and remind him that he must remain in a sitting position for more than a few seconds!

As training progresses, you may wait for longer intervals before giving him the tidbit, and eventually replace the food reward with praise.

Down

Teach Lotus to lie down by starting him in a sitting position. Kneel down alongside of him, on his righthand side, facing the same direction, and rest your hand lightly on his shoulders. If it is more comfortable for you to stand, and if Lotus is accustomed to a grooming table, you can teach him the *down* command on the table, so you won't have to kneel down on the ground. Show Lotus a food reward and then slowly lower the food to the ground (or table surface) on which he is standing. This should encourage him to lie down to reach the food, but in the beginning you

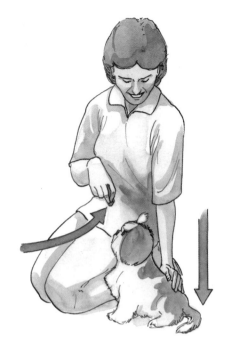

Sit is the easiest command to learn. As your puppy's nose goes up to follow the tidbit, the hindquarters will drop into a sitting position. Be sure to give your puppy lots of praise.

may have to apply light pressure to the top of his shoulders or pull one front leg gently out in front of him. Once Lotus is in the *down* position, praise him and give him a food reward. As with other commands, you will eventually replace the food reward with praise alone.

Stay

Stay is a tough command for Shih Tzus, especially Shih Tzus like yours that want to be the center of attention and where all the activity is. Remember that your pet was bred to stay close to you and in your presence almost all of the time. Asking

Lotus to *stay* somewhere else while you walk away or take leave will be confusing and upsetting to him. He will want to get up and follow you immediately and his feelings may be hurt if you are too harsh when you tell him to *stay*. In the beginning, Lotus should be expected to *stay* in place for only a very short time period.

Don't try to teach Lotus to *stay* until he has learned the *sit* and *down* commands very well. You don't want to add chaos to confusion or to undo the successful training you have already accomplished. At first Lotus will be confused by your command

Your Shih Tzu can learn the stay *command in the sit or down position.* Stay *is an important command, but it can take longer to learn than other commands, so be patient and reward your pet as it learns.*

because for most of his early training you have been asking him to come to you. Now you are going to ask him to remain where he is. It won't make a bit of sense to him.

Stay is an important command that Lotus should learn. It can be very handy in an emergency situation. Be patient and work in small steps; little by little, Lotus will understand what you want him to do.

Note: To avoid injury, do not teach Lotus this command on the tabletop. He will not always obey your *stay* command and might jump off the table and be injured.

• To teach Lotus to *stay,* make him lie down on the floor. While placing your hand firmly on top of his shoulders, tell him to *stay*. For the first few training sessions, if Lotus remains in place with your hand on his shoulders for 30 seconds, he deserves lots of praise. If he is still for a full minute, a food reward might be in order!

• For the next several lessons, make Lotus lie down and tell him to *stay,* then back away from him about 3 feet (1 m) and wait one minute. If he jumps up to run to you, gently return him to his assigned place and tell him to *stay,* while simultaneously keeping your hand on his shoulder.

• After Lotus has learned to *stay* in place for one minute with you seated a few feet in front of him, begin to lengthen the time period as well as your distance from him. If he starts to leave his designated spot, tell him to *stay* and raise your hand so that the palm of your hand is facing him. It won't take him long to associate the word with the hand signal and to understand that he is to remain in place until you call him and praise him for his good behavior.

Lotus might become very bored with this command, so keep training sessions to only a few minutes. If he becomes too bored he might become belligerent and no longer want to behave. You will have taken three steps backward for the one step forward in your training. Watch closely for signs of boredom or annoyance and stop the training before it reaches that point. Be sure to bring the session to a close immediately after one of the times Lotus has done what you have asked of him and not after he has done something incorrectly or, worse yet, refused to do what you asked him to do.

Leash Training

After you have trained Lotus to come when called and to follow you around the yard, you are ready to begin leash training.

• Begin by attaching a light line, such as string or yarn, to his harness and allow him to drag the line behind him and to play with it. Encourage him to follow you with the string dangling along.

• When he has become accustomed to the string, replace it with the leash. Lotus will quickly adapt to the leash dragging on the ground, and when

he has, you can then pick it up and walk with him.

• Begin by holding the leash and following Lotus wherever he goes. This way he will not fight the leash or consider it a threat. He probably will ignore it.

• As your training sessions progress, you will begin to guide your pet. Decide where you want to go, and with Lotus on the leash, encourage him with words and praise to follow you to that location. In the beginning the distance should be short, maybe just halfway across the backyard. If Lotus elects not to come along, simply stop where you are and wait. *Don't drag him or pull on him.* He may struggle against the leash at first, trying to get away, but he will quickly learn that any pulling or discomfort is created by his own activities and there is no resistance if he follows you. As soon as Lotus gives up the fight and approaches you or follows you, praise him for his common sense and end the training session shortly thereafter on a positive note with a food reward.

With patience, praise, and consistency in training, Lotus will be following along on the leash in no time. He may weave a bit, or run a little ahead, or drop behind for a moment to investigate something interesting on the ground, but he now will have the general idea. Once he reaches this level in his leash training, you can begin to work on fine-tuning him to *heel.*

Chapter Ten
The Talented Shih Tzu

Shih Tzus are not only charming, affectionate companions; they are attractive, clever, and dynamic. They can learn to do a lot of things but they excel at the things they were bred to do: showing off their good looks and bringing joy to those who know them. So let's take a look at some of the fun ways you can put Lotus's talents to the test!

Dog Shows

Dog shows are a lot of fun for both exhibitors and observers. Dogs are judged on how closely they come to the ideal standard for conformation for their breeds. If Lotus is handsome enough to compete against the best of his breed, consider joining a Shih Tzu club, as well as a local kennel club. These clubs can provide you with information on show dates and locations, judges, professional handlers, and canine activities, and even offer handling classes to teach you and your dog the ropes. Dog clubs also organize fun matches—dog shows where you can practice and perfect what you've learned before you participate in an all-breed or

specialty (one breed only, in your case, Shih Tzus) show.

Fun Matches

You can prepare yourself and your puppy for a future in the conformation ring by attending fun matches. Fun matches are just that—fun! They are hosted by American Kennel Club (AKC)-approved breed clubs and are conducted according to AKC show rules. Only purebred, AKC-registered dogs may participate. However, fun matches do not count toward points for a championship and dogs that have won points toward a championship do not compete. Judges at fun matches may be official AKC judges, or knowledgeable dog breeders or handlers selected by the hosting club. Fun matches are a great way for you and your puppy to practice all aspects of a real dog show, from traveling to grooming, to exhibiting, to winning!

Specialty Shows

Under the AKC show regulations, there are two types of conformation shows. They are specialty and group

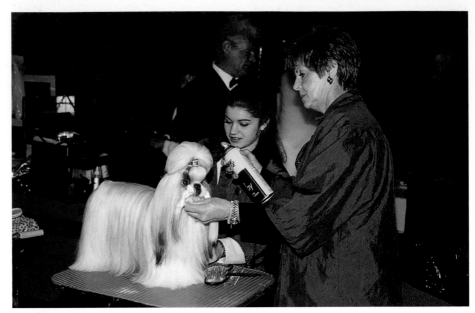

Every Shih Tzu must look its best when it competes. Shih Tzu exhibitors spend hours preparing their fancy canines to perfection before entering the show ring.

shows, and all-breed shows. Dogs are judged according to their breed standard and, by a process of elimination, one dog is selected as Best of Breed.

A specialty show is limited to a designated breed or grouping of breeds. For example, the Shih Tzu Club of America holds an annual show for Shih Tzus only. The show is held under AKC rules by the individual breed clubs.

The Shih Tzu Club of America is responsible for maintaining the official standards of the breed. If there are any changes or revisions to be made, the club must approve them before submitting them for final approval to the AKC.

To become a champion, a Shih Tzu must win a minimum of 15 points by competing in formal American Kennel Club-sanctioned, licensed events. The points must be accumulated as major wins under different judges.

All-Breed Shows

As the name implies, all-breed shows are for all different breeds. Judging is conducted according to AKC rules. In addition to Best of Breed winners, Open shows offer the titles of Best in Group (for dogs considered to be the best representative of their group) and Best in Show (for the dog selected as the best representative of its breed and group, compared to all other dogs of other breeds and groups).

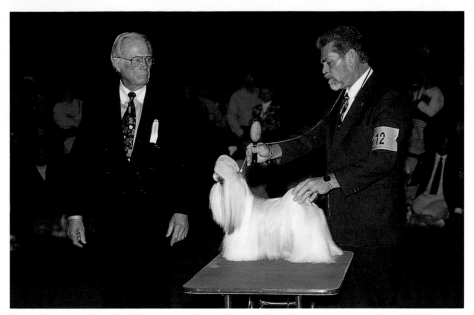

Dog shows are fun, but the competition is fierce. Dog shows are for serious Shih Tzu connoisseurs!

Most dogs competing in Specialty or Open shows are competing for points toward their championship. A dog can earn from one to five points at a show. The number of points available depends upon the number of entries. Wins of three, four, or five points are called "majors." The fifteen points required for a championship title must be won under at least three different judges and include two majors won under two different judges.

There are five different classes in which a dog can compete for championship points and the classes are divided by sex:
• Puppy class (divided into 6–9 months of age and 9–12 months of age)

• Novice
• Bred by exhibitor
• American-bred
• Open

Male dogs are judged first in this order: Puppy dogs, Novice dogs, Bred by Exhibitor dogs, American-bred dogs, and Open dogs. The first-place winners in each class later return to the ring to compete against each other. This class is called the Winners Class. The dog selected as the best male in the Winners Class is the Winners Dog. This is the dog that will win the championship points in the show. The male that placed second to the Winners Dog that was in the Winners Dog's original class (that is, Puppy, Novice, Bred by Exhibitor, American-bred, or Open) is then brought in to join the Winners Class to compete against the remaining four dogs in the class. The dog that wins second place winner in the Winners Class is the Reserve Winners Dog. If, for any reason, the AKC disallows the championship points to the Winners Dog, the Reserve Winners Dog will receive the points. The same procedure is then followed, in the same order, for the females, and the Winners Bitch (that also wins championship points) and Reserve Winners Bitch are selected.

Best of Breed

The Winners Dog and Winners Bitch then compete in a class called the Best of Breed. Entered in this class are dogs and bitches that already have won their championship titles. The judge selects either the Winners Dog or the Winners Bitch to be Best of Winners. Then the judge selects an animal from the group to be Best of Breed. If the Best of Breed winner is a male, the judge selects the best bitch to be Best of Opposite Sex to the Best of Winners. If the Best of Breed winner is a female, the judge selects a male for Best of Opposite Sex to the Best of Winners.

At an all-breed show, judging takes place for each breed, then each Best of Breed winner competes in its breed group. The seven breed groups are:

1. Sporting group
2. Hound group
3. Working group
4. Terrier group
5. Toy group
6. Non-sporting group
7. Herding group

The first-place winners of each breed group then compete against each other for the coveted title of Best in Show.

Obedience Trials

Yes, Shih Tzus compete in obedience and they do well, too! Your little "lion dog" is as smart as he looks and he is eager to prove it. The trick is keeping his attention long enough to make sure he knows exactly what it is you want him to do. Of course, Shih Tzus love to play, so make the training sessions fun and turn them into games followed by lots of praise. Your future "companion dog excellent" will do everything he can to earn your love and attention. In obedience competitions it's intelligence that counts—both human and canine! Your dog is smart enough to learn the commands and you must be clever enough to find a method that works for both of you. You must be able to get your Shih Tzu's attention, keep his attention, motivate him, and teach him what to do without confusing him. It's a challenge, but one you and Lotus can meet.

In obedience trials dogs are put through a series of exercises and commands and judged according to how well they do. Each dog starts out with 200 points. Points are subtracted throughout the trials or tests for lack of attention, nonperformance, barking, or slowness.

The Shih Tzu has left an indelible footprint in the hearts of admirers worldwide.

Obedience trials are divided into three levels; each progressive level is more difficult and challenging:
• Novice—Companion Dog (CD)
• Open—Companion Dog Excellent (CDX)
• Utility—Utility Dog (UD) and Utility Dog Excellent (UDX)

To earn a CD title, Lotus must be able to perform six exercises: *heel* on leash, *stand* for examination, *heel* free, *recall,* long *sit,* and long *down.*

To earn a CDX title he must be able to *heel* free, drop on *recall, retrieve* on flat, *retrieve* over the high jump, *broad jump,* long *sit,* and long *down.*

To earn a UD, Lotus must respond to signal exercise, scent discrimina-tion tests, directed retrieve, directed jumping, and group examination.

Lotus must earn three legs to receive his title. To receive a leg he has to earn at least 170 points out of a possible perfect score of 200, and receive more than 50 percent on each exercise.

What does it take to earn a UDX, the toughest and most coveted of all obedience titles? The dog and its trainer/handler must pass the Open and Utility classes on the same day. Could a Shih Tzu accomplish such a feat? Absolutely. In 1998 a Shih Tzu earned the UDX for the first time in the history of the breed. Now it's your turn!

Agility Competitions

Agility competitions are lots of fun and extremely popular. They are timed events that are exciting and fast-paced. Dogs complete challenging obstacle courses, jump over objects, teeter on seesaws, cross bridges, run through tunnels, and weave in and out between poles. Titles to be earned, in increasing level of difficulty, are: Novice Agility (NA), Open Agility (OA), Agility Excellent (AX), and Master Agility Excellent (MX).

Shih Tzus can be very entertaining at agility competitions. They are dynamic, sturdy, well-muscled dogs that are physically capable of agility work. And Shih Tzus are keen competitors that love every second of the course. Some have been known to have so much fun that they repeat the obstacles more times than required. Unfortunately, there are no extra points for such exuberance! But most Shih Tzus follow directions well and enthusiastically and they are rewarded with well-earned titles.

Games

Shih Tzus enjoy all kinds of games, from hide-and-seek to fetch. Spry, lively, dynamic, and full of fun, your Shih Tzu will surprise and delight you with his ingenuity and creativity.

Obedient Servant

Not all Shih Tzus live the life of luxury. Many are very hard workers, serving as pet-facilitated therapy animals, bringing joy to people in hospitals. They also work as hearing dogs.

As pets for the hearing impaired, Shih Tzus alert their owners to sounds such as the ring of a doorbell or telephone, a timer, a baby crying, fire and smoke alarms, or a prowler. The Shih Tzu may be a little dog, but for the Shih Tzu who loves his owner, no job is too big.

The Quintessential Canine

From ancient temples to your cozy home, from the brink of extinction to Best in Show winner, from pampered pet to hard worker, the Shih Tzu is a most remarkable dog that has succeeded against all odds. It's no wonder that this attractive, charming, little dog is happy whether in the show ring or in your lap. Devoted and trusting, full of fun and full of affection, the Shih Tzu is truly the quintessential canine companion. It deserves its status today as an adored pet worldwide.

So the next time you sit down to snuggle with your Shih Tzu and look into those big, beautiful eyes and find you are smitten, don't worry. For thousands of years, thousands of people from all walks of life have felt the same way you do. You're in good company!

Useful Literature and Web Sites

Kennel and Breed Clubs

American Shih Tzu Club, Inc.
Bonnie Prato,
    Corresponding Secretary
5252 Shafter Avenue
Oakland, CA 94618
www.shihtzu.org

American Kennel Club (AKC)
Registrations
5580 Centerview Drive
Raleigh, NC 27606-3390
(919) 233-9767
www.akc.org

The Canadian Kennel Club
89 Skyway Avenue, Suite 100
Etobicoke, Ontario, Canada
M9W6R4
(416) 675-5511

Fédération Cynologique
    Internationale
Secretariat Général de la FCA
Place Albert 1er, 13
B-6530 Thuin, Belgium
www.fci.be/english

The Kennel Club
1-4 Clargis Street, Picadilly
London W7Y 8AB, England

States Kennel Club
1007 W. Pine Street
Hattiesburg, MS 39401
(601) 583-8345

United Kennel Club (UKC)
100 East Kilgore Road
Kalamazoo, MI 49001-5598
(616) 343-9020

United States Dog Agility Association
P.O. Box 850955
Richardson, TX 75085-8955
(972) 231-9700
Fax: (214) 503-0161
E-mail: *info@usdaa.com*
www.usdaa.com

Health-related Associations and Foundations

AKC Canine Health Foundation
251 W. Garfield Road
Aurora, OH 44202
(216) 995-0806
akchf@aol.com

American Society for the Prevention
    of Cruelty to Animals (ASPCA)
424 East 92nd Street
New York, NY 10128-6804
(212) 876-7700
www.aspca.org

American Veterinary Medical
  Association (AVMA)
930 North Meacham Road
Schaumberg, IL 60173
(847) 925-8070
www.avma.org

Canine Eye Registration Foundation
  (CERF)
South Campus Court, Building C
West Lafayette, IN 47907
(765) 494-8179

Dogs for the Deaf
10175 Wheeler Road
Central Point, OR 97502
(541) 826-9220
E-mail: *info@dogsforthedeaf.org*
www.dogsforthedeaf.org

Institute for Genetic Disease Control
  in Animals
P.O. Box 177
Warner, NH 03278
(603) 456-2350
*www.vetmed.ucdavis.edu/gdc/
  gdc.htm*

International Canine Semen Bank
P.O. Box 651
Sandy, OR 97055
(503) 663-7031

National Animal Poison Control
  Center (NAPCC)
Animal Product Safety Service
1717 South Philo Road, Suite 36
Urbana, IL 61802
(888) 4ANI-HELP
(888) 426-4435
(900) 680-0000
(Consultation fees apply; call for details)
www.napcc.aspca.org

Orthopedic Foundation for Animals
  (OFA)
2300 Nifong Boulevard
Columbia, MO 65201
www.offa.org

Lost Pet Registries
The American Kennel Club (AKC)
AKC Companion Recovery
5580 Centerview Drive, Suite 250
Raleigh, NC 27606-3394
(800) 252-7894
E-mail: *found@akc.org*
www.akc.org/car.htm

Home Again Microchip Service
(800) LONELY-ONE

National Dog Registry (NDR)
P.O. Box 118
Woodstock, NY 12498-0116
(800) 637-3647

Petfinders
368 High Street
Athol, NY 12810
(800) 223-4747

Periodicals
*The American Kennel Club
  Gazette*
51 Madison Avenue
New York, NY 10010
(800) 490-5675
www.akc.org

Dog Fancy
Subscription Division
P.O. Box 53264
Boulder, CO 80322-3264
(303) 786-7306/666-8504
www.dogfancy.com

Shih Tzus come in a variety of colors and markings.

Dogs USA Annual
P.O. Box 6050
Mission Viejo, CA 92690-6050
(800) 855-8822

Dog World
29 North Wacker Drive
Chicago, IL 60606
(312) 726-2802

Books

The Complete Dog Book, Official Publication of the American Kennel Club. New York, NY: Howell Book House, 1992.

Dadds, Audrey. *The Shih Tzu*. New York, NY: Howell Book House, 1976.

Dunbar, Ian. *The Essential Shih Tzu*. New York, NY: Howell Book House, 1999.

Joris, Victor. *The Complete Shih Tzu*. New York, NY: Howell Book House, 1994.

Sucher, Jaime. *Shih Tzus: A Complete Pet Owner's Manual*. Hauppauge, New York: Barron's Educational Series, Inc., 2000.

White, Jo Ann. *The Official Book of the Shih Tzu*. Neptune City, NJ: T.F.H. Publications, 1995.

What do these pups have in common? As Shih Tzus became extinct in China, a few survivors were imported to the United Kingdom. The Shetland Sheepdog and West Highland White Terrier are United Kingdom natives.

Your pet will depend on you for everything for its entire life. Are you ready for such a big commitment?

Index